MW01248955

I'm grateful that Terry has shared
bility as he shares his heartache is
Christians "live in the now, and the not yet."
shown in Terry's struggle to connect with God and cope through his many
griefs. Terry's life experience is a living example of how pain and suffering
can lead to hope and healing. Hearing his challenge to apply God's promises and focus on gratitude is an inspiration. His experience of how his community and God strengthened him (like a "woven cord, hard to break") is
an important reminder to come alongside people in practical ways when
life is hard. In my line of work and in my own health journey, I experience
suffering. Terry's story gives some insight into how it is possible, as he says,
to "open the curtains, crank open the window, and let the sunshine in."

This is a must-read account for anyone going through tough times. Hearing his story will likely help to build your own faith that since God helped
him through, it's possible that He could do something similar in your life.

—Brett Ullman, author of *Parenting: Navigating Everything*

This is for all who've been blindsided by pain too deep to trust to social
media, who long for refuge in the storm, for hope in despair. It's a pearl
of a story from an honest guy who dares to grapple and ask and somehow
believe that prayer can poke holes in the sky so some light can shine
through.

—Phil Callaway, radio host and author of *Laugh Like a Kid Again*

God promises to take our worst and darkest moments and make from
them something beautiful. Most of us have to take that on faith. But once
in a rare while, an artist comes along who gives us language for it, who
spies the pattern in the chaos, who sees the hand of God at work within
the pain and loss and sadness, and who wrests from that a testimony of
radiant hope. Terry Posthumus is that artist. This book is that testimony.

—Mark Buchanan, author of *David: Rise*

Everybody has a story, of course, but few could match the dramatic twists
and turns of the story told in this small volume. From the first paragraph
you will experience the loss and gain, the challenge and triumph, the

mystery and wonder of real life unpredictably unpacked on every page. You will meet Terry Posthumus, a most extraordinary man. And you meet an astonishing God who can redeem and bless. I know Terry. His testimony is altogether legit. And I know his faith. Authentic and true. Don't walk by this read. It can reframe even your story.

—Jim Lyon, general director, Church of God Ministries for the United States and Canada

Terry calls this poignant book a "memoir with a purpose," and I know that readers, like me, who have experienced seasons of deep grief will be encouraged. Through deeply personal and unflinchingly honest stories, Terry has opened his broken heart and shows us how healing it is when we listen for God's comforting voice even in moments of pain; blame is replaced by compassion, anger by love, and despair by hope.

—Michael Messenger, president and CEO, World Vision Canada

Hope! In a season when hope seems in short supply, Terry invites you to journey with him into hope. On this journey you will discover that hope is not an empty wish, nor does it require you to dig deep into your tired or beaten soul to conjure up more. It is an easy thing to lose our hope (and joy) when life beats up on us. Hope is found in the Jesus-journey. Terry discovered that Jesus was always with him, even in very dark places, and each chapter reminds us of the hope we can have.

—Rev. Dr. Cliff Fletcher, bishop of The Free Methodist Church in Canada

Terry Posthumus is a rarity ... Terry is an extremely talented artist, musician, and storyteller, and while he's often the most well-read guy in the room, he likes to listen more than he talks. He's one of the most engaging and down-to-earth performers I've ever had the privilege to work with ... it's kind of irritating. In all earnest ... buy this book!

—Steve Geyer, comic, author, and all-around decent fellow

ACQUAINTED WITH SORROW

WHEN YOUR LIFE FEELS LIKE THE WORST IS YET TO COME

TERRY POSTHUMUS

Published by Castle Quay Books
Burlington, Ontario, Canada and Jupiter, Florida, U.S.A.
416-573-3249 | info@castlequaybooks.com | www.castlequaybooks.com

Edited by Marina Hofman Willard
Front cover design by www.terryposthumus.com
Book interior by Burst Impressions

Printed in Canada.

Library and Archives Canada Cataloguing in Publication

Title: Acquainted with sorrow : when your life feels like the worst is yet to come / by Terry Posthumus.
Names: Posthumus, Terry, author.
Identifiers: Canadiana 2022026967X | ISBN 9781988928692 (softcover)
Subjects: LCSH: Despair—Religious aspects—Christianity. | LCSH: Grief—Religious aspects—
Christianity. | LCSH: Hope—Religious aspects—Christianity.
Classification: LCC BT774.5 .P67 2022 | DDC 248.8/6—dc23

CASTLE QUAY BOOKS

Foreword I

Hope. Perhaps the most elusive emotion of any we experience. It is undeniably transformative. It is affected by external circumstances. It is contagious. It alters the trajectory of our life. It grows with exercise. And it always requires a choice. It seems that the circumstances of a broken and fallen world conspire against the human heart to rob it of hope and a future. Yet in the kingdom economy, God has provided a currency that transforms both the direction of our lives as well as the very journey on the way. As with everything that God makes available to us, it is never forced, only offered. The hope before us requires a choice and daily nurture to grow and mature. It flowers into a life of vibrancy and flourishing irrespective of the circumstances. That certainly doesn't mean that it is easy. And some mistake hope for a form of optimism. But for the humble Christ follower, choosing hope over despair is a willful act of faith—trusting in the author of life to bring good out of pain, joy out of sorrow. In the process, all of it becomes part of our journey toward being fully human as God envisioned us to be.

If you have ever reflected upon your life, likely you have recognized the very real possibility for despair. It is easy to understand how despair can lead us to dismal places and apparent dead ends. Every day we make choices that are life or death. Life-or-death choices do not necessarily mean that someone's very life hangs in the balance. It's not that each day we choose whether or not someone lives or dies. I don't mean that we are always in a life-or-death situation. But we make life-or-death decisions each day in the smallest matters. When we close off the possibility of grace, when we deny the opportunity for forgiveness, when we ignore God's involvement in bringing good from ashes, or when we live under the circumstances believing there is no hope, then we are making choices for death. We abort the possibility of God's great love transforming dismal circumstances into vibrant life.

When we leave open the possibility for reconciliation, when we allow for a spark of light to be infused into an otherwise dark circumstance, when we invite the life-giving Holy Spirit into troubled relationships, and when we allow our hearts to rest in the generative love of God, then we are choosing hope. When we choose hope, we are choosing life.

My prayer is that in reading Terry's story in this book, you will be inspired. More than that, I pray that you will be compelled to begin the journey marked by hopeful choices. Among Christ followers, that trajectory is marked by the generosity of fellow Christians surrounding, uplifting, and encouraging you in community. Choosing hope sets your life on a new trajectory. Choosing hope gives those around you the opportunity to become the hands and feet of Jesus. Choosing hope makes God smile!

—Rev. Kevin Mannoia, Ph.D, former president of National Association of Evangelicals, former bishop of Free Methodist Church-USA, former dean of Azusa Pacific University School of Theology, and president of International Council of Higher Education

Foreword II

For the last decade, I have played a lot of music with Terry—writing songs, recording, touring—and I've heard Terry share his story on countless occasions. While it's easy to become overwhelmed by the sad and heartbreaking events, Terry never fails to guide the listener through the sorrow to the One who guides him—to Jesus.

In Psalm 71, the writer prays for God to take his hand and deliver him. He prays this because he knows that God *can* deliver him. His trust is rooted in his experience of God who "has been his hope" (Psalm 71:5). The source of his confidence is not a function of his own best effort or positive outlook; it isn't a result of his persuasive words or gritty determination. It is because he is the recipient of God's gift of hope—the certainty that God is good and that His love endures forever.

And that's why the psalmist confidently declares: "As for me, I will always have hope; I will praise you more and more" (Psalm 71:14). The writer is fully aware of God's gift of hope—an "always" hope, an *unbroken* hope—which leads him to praise. And he knows that the outpouring of praise enriches his experience of God's hope. The "more and more" of praise resonates with the "always" of hope.

Whenever I hear Terry share his story, I hear echoes of Psalm 71. And the richness of God's hope reverberates in the caverns of my own experience of sorrow and heartbreak. Terry embraces the inexplicable link between the gift of hope and the work of praise, receiving with one hand while giving with the other. All the while, leading us to Jesus.

Here, in this book, Terry does his part to extend the reach of God's hand of hope to each of us. May you be led to the One who is our hope.

—Ken Michell, MTS, DWS, lecturer, music and worship arts, Tyndale University

Contents

Acknowledgements

Thank you so much to my wife and best friend, Jessica, who was instrumental in getting me to write this book! When I was grumpy, you were patient. When I lacked confidence, you encouraged me. You came alongside me and pointed me back in the right direction when I got off track. God has opened my eyes to love in a whole new way by bringing us together, and I'm glad we get to walk through this life as one.

To my children who are with me: Theo, Justin, Kara, Nicholas, Karissa, Michael, Lara, Jayme, Elissa, Catherine, and Bella, who bring so much joy into my life at various times and in sundry ways. I love you, and I am proud to be your father. Being your dad has taught me how God loves us, His children.

To Dr. Tony Campolo for encouraging me to write this book. Our meeting at Tim Horton's was exactly what I needed to get going in the process of writing these stories and pointing people to hope.

To Dr. Kevin Mannoia for coaching and mentoring me through the entire writing process. I am thankful for the timely, creative, and practical advice you shared because I might never have begun writing without it.

To Larry Willard for walking this first-time author through the steps and processes of publishing. Thank you for encouraging me to enter my manuscript into the Word Guild Awards and guiding me through the release of this book.

To Rob Clement for being an adviser and a sounding board. Thank you for your kindness and friendship.

To Steve Bell, for being an encourager and a friend. Thank you for edifying me with your sage wisdom and kindness.

To Mark Buchanan, for being an adviser and sounding board as I wound my way through the process of writing.

To Ken Michel, for your stalwart friendship and your editing skills. You took these roughly hewn ideas and helped me hone the edges and polish the sheen.

To Lorraine Posthumus, though you are no longer with us, your testimony of faith, hope, and love lives on through these stories. Our past together helped shape me into the man I am today, and I am thankful for the time we shared and the beautiful stories that come from it.

My children who have preceded me into heaven, Gracie, Cherie, and Ezekiel Posthumus. Your departures, although heartbreaking, have become much of the impetus behind these stories of hope.

A Note from the Author

Our experiences shape us into who we are. They are not merely events on our timeline. The things we go through affect us profoundly and form how we view and react to our present and future circumstances.

I'm a man who has experienced many different types of loss and grief. From the time I was a child and on into my adult years, I have known sorrow. I am well acquainted with grief.

And yet, these events and experiences have not destroyed me. I'm not a sad or bitter person. Quite the opposite. I would describe myself as hopeful, peaceful, joyful, and loved despite the deep sorrow I have known.

This raises the question, "How can that be?" For that, I have but one answer.

Simple. My faith in Jesus.

I know that Jesus gets it because He was the original Man of Sorrows. Isaiah wrote about it when he prophesied about our Redeemer: "He was … a man of deep sorrows who was no stranger to suffering and grief" (Isaiah 53:3 TPT).

Reading this, I know that Jesus feels my pain. He understands my suffering and grief, and I'm comforted.

Long before I even existed, Jesus took my burden, which is heavy, and offered me His, which is light. And when all is said and done, He has transformed despair into hope, tumult into peace, sorrow into joy, and bitterness into love.

And that's the reason I wrote this book.

I've been given hope despite shocking loss and grief. I hope to provide you with a window into my soul's most vulnerable state through this book. Opening the window to my heart, I hope that these stories will have a profound and lasting impact as hope takes pre-eminence over despair.

I explore many themes in this book, including sorrow, grief, faith, resiliency, and betrayal, but hope is the overarching and predominant theme. I encourage you to look at your life through the filter of hope—the hope that comes from believing in Jesus.

You may find it challenging to take in all the stories as you read this book. The stories are, at times, traumatic and heartbreaking and, at other times, celebratory. If you're prone to tears, you might want to keep a box of tissues close by.

As you read through this book, you may find yourself emotionally drained—in the best way possible. I hope that reading these stories will make you feel grateful and amazed at God's goodness despite the storms of life.

I've woven many Bible stories into the narrative of this book. These stories have significantly impacted my life. I hope they become alive and relevant to you, that you're able to see the connection between these Bible stories and my experiences, and that the Word of God becomes life to you.

I want to clarify that I have survived—and even thrived—despite my story because of what Jesus did for me. He is with you on this journey of life. Include Him in your story because He will walk with you through anything and everything.

My prayer for you is that after reading this memoir, you will have a closer and deeper relationship with God.

Introduction

A Bridge

The figure of a man emerged from gloom and shadows.
He slept under a bridge in what amounted to a burlap sack.

The bridge was a decaying wood and steel antique that spanned railroad tracks. It was not safe, not for people anyway. The roadway above provided shelter from the elements, but it was a dirty and dangerous place. It was never meant to be a shelter for humans.

It wasn't quiet—trains roared by all the time, day and night. Cars passed overhead, producing a deafening roar. There was no peace under the bridge. Secluded and hidden from view, this place was the last resort for the discarded, the desperate, and the downtrodden.

Under the bridge, the chilled air was damp. There was no sun to offer warmth. The cold was relentless, and there was no escaping it.

The man wore the sum of everything he owned. Describing his appearance as unkempt would be an understatement.

Nobody knows where he came from or how he ended up living under a bridge. Most folks give him a wide berth. They see him as surly, sullen, and soiled. People avoid the dishevelled, solitary man who lives under the bridge.

It could be me. It could be any of us. We're all one or two bad decisions from being in the same place.

Under a bridge.

A Window

While sharing a meal with my friends, Kevin and Kathy, I told them about the losses I've suffered over the years. Astonished, Kathy asked, "How is it that you don't live under a bridge somewhere?" Kevin jumped in as I mulled her question over, "He decided to open the curtains and let the sunshine in."

Kevin's comment resonated with me, and I found myself thinking about it. The way he put it stuck with me. He said it was a decision, which means there were options. To choose between darkness and light, despair and hope.

Open the curtains—let the sunshine in—let hope shine in.

I hadn't thought of it, but it's a miracle that I don't live under a bridge somewhere—drunk or worse. I've never contemplated running from my life. I still have hope. And I don't feel like I'm gutsy or brave. The light of hope is a gift. It's not something I mustered myself.

A Rope

Two of my sons clean windows on high-rise buildings. The idea of it makes my stomach lurch. I'm not good with heights.

When you work a job like theirs, safety is paramount. Strapped into a safety harness and secured with ropes more than strong enough to bear their weight, they're safe. They're also protected by a safety backup line with ample strength to catch them should they start to fall.

When I reflect on my life, I can relate to the idea of safety and having a rope to catch me should I begin to fall.

"A rope that is woven of three strings is hard to break" (Ecclesiastes 4:12 NCV).

On my own, I'm easily defeated. In a community of God-fearing people, I'm defended. Add the steady hand of a loving and faithful God, and I'm like a woven cord, hard to break.

As you read, bear a few things in mind. This book tells my story about loss. It's a memoir with a purpose. And the intention is that you might find some comfort or encouragement in life's darkest moments.

I've been there. I'm well acquainted with sorrow. I've also had experiences that have kindled the light of hope.

I've wrestled with faith and trust in God in the darkest moments. I've collapsed under the overwhelming weight. I know what it feels like to have my heart shattered. I've felt the fire of anger toward God and questioned the "fairness" of the deep losses I've suffered.

I've also experienced the closeness of friends and the wonder of a heart that begins beating again after I thought it had died. That heart was mine.

This book does not provide a map or formula for dealing with loss and grief. My experiences are simply my experiences. I am not trying to tell you that you'll have the same result if you do what I did. Instead, I'm trying to say that there's a good reason to hang on to hope. Or maybe to grasp it for the first time. I want to point you to the One who gives hope. True hope.

If one chapter or season of my life doesn't resonate with you, or worse, makes you angry, please don't give up on the story. I've experienced different types of losses and grief during different seasons of my life. Each story is different, and each experience showed me how God's grace is expansive and consistent. He is the solution to anything and everything.

May you see your loving Father in this book, and may you find yourself safe in His caring and protecting hands.

As you read, may you discover a deeper sense of hope and in doing so, may you be able to walk away from under the bridge. May you throw back the curtains, open a window, and let light push back the darkness. And may these stories of hope be a lifeline to grab on to if you find yourself falling.

Chapter 1
Fatherless Child

"Great is Thy faithfulness," O God my Father,
There is no shadow of turning with Thee;
Thou changest not, Thy compassions, they fail not
As Thou hast been, Thou forever wilt be.
(Thomas O. Chisholm)

It's hard for a little boy to grow up without his dad. My father was killed when I was five. The morning my father died, I went to school like any other day. When I came home at lunch, he was gone—for good.

I don't have many memories of that day—just three.

The first was the number of people in my house. Ministers. Relatives. Friends. Strangers. All of them were there to comfort my mom and help us in any way they could.

The second memory is that I got to go to my friend Gordie's house. I loved going there. He was really cool.

The third was a candy bar I was given—and I didn't have to share it with anybody—my own chocolate bar.

Although I cannot remember much of the day my father was killed, I have many memories from the weeks, months, and years that followed. My mom raised us on her own for four years—a widow with three young children.

It was hard for this little boy to grow up without his father. Sure. But during this time, I began to recognize God as my father, and I realized that He could be trusted.

The Widow of Zarephath

There was a widow who lived in Zarephath during the reign of Ahab. At the time of this story, there was famine. Widows were some of the poorest people in the ancient world. This woman would likely have been one of the first to run out of food during a drought.

In 1 Kings 17, the prophet Elijah was riding out the famine. Living by a stream, he had water. He didn't have access to Uber Eats, but ravens brought him food twice daily. Morning and evening—like clockwork.

As it happens, he didn't end up at the stream by chance. Elijah had been directed there by God, and the ravens had been commanded to feed him.

As the drought wore on, the stream dried up—and it was time for another directive from God.

He told Elijah to move to Zarephath. God told him He had commanded a widow from there to take care of his needs. So Elijah packed up his things and headed out.

The story says that as Elijah reached the town gate, he saw a woman gathering wood. Thirsty, he asked her, "Would you mind getting me a drink of water?" As she headed off to get him a drink, he said, "And a piece of bread, too."

She answered, "I don't have any food. I swear." Then she said, "I was out here collecting wood so I could prepare a final meal. It'll be the last food my son and I eat before we die. I have a bit of flour and oil. That's it. After it's gone, we're done."

Unfazed by the woman's dire report, Elijah said, "Go ahead. But before you do, make me a small loaf of bread. Then, make the meal for you and your son."

Then he added, "The Lord, the God of Israel, says, 'The jar of flour will not be used up and the jug of oil will not run dry until the day the Lord sends rain on the land" (1 Kings 17:14).

Her response? Faith that led to obedience. She did what Elijah told her to do. She put God's interests before her own.

God's response? "There was food every day for Elijah and for the woman and her family. For the jar of flour was not used up and the jug of oil did not run dry, in keeping with the word of the Lord spoken by Elijah." (1 Kings 17:15–16).

I know this kind of story firsthand. A widow. Her children. A sugar bowl that never runs out.

Wait. What?

The Sugar Bowl

My mom had this coffee service set on our kitchen counter. It was purely decorative.

When I say purely decorative, I mean from a coffee service point of view. The set was used to store things it was not created to hold. Receipts, bobby pins, safety pins, and stray fasteners of mysterious origin could be found in the cups and coffee pot that came with the set. This was my mom's version of a "junk drawer."

The sugar bowl in the set was the outlier. Whereas the other vessels could be used for a myriad of storage needs, the sugar bowl was reserved for cash—hairdressing money, to be exact.

Mom was a hairdresser, and from my earliest memories, I can recall her doing hair in our home. She had all the regulars who came on Friday for their weekend "wash and sets" and "updos." Some came for perms and some for haircuts. Our kitchen served as a nifty little hair salon.

My mom ran a pretty tight ship. Her setup was minimal and optimal. Her routine was methodical and memorable.

The customer arrived and settled in. Out came the blue hard-shell carry-on suitcase she used to store the tools of her trade. After opening the case, she pulled out the cape with flair, and the beautification ensued. Her customers might walk in dishevelled and in various mood states, but they left impeccably coiffed and cheered up. Mom was a good hairdresser and an engaging conversationalist.

When I think back on my childhood, many of the images of my mom include her standing behind one of her customers with a comb in her hand and bobby pins in her teeth. If there were a soundtrack to accompany the memories, it would be composed of chatter and laughter.

That's how my mom supported my siblings and me during her years as a widow.

My father had been a young independent businessman. He was twenty-six years old when he died, so there wasn't a massive amount of savings for my mom to live off. The two of them were just getting started in life. Without a significant life insurance policy, there wasn't any kind of financial bailout available for our family.

This left us in a very precarious position. On the day my dad died, my mom became the sole source of income (other than a small widow's pension) for our household.

Mom had to rely on faith, family, church community, and her own hands. That's what she did. From my perspective, she exemplified the "work as if it depends on you; pray as if it depends on God" from my perspective. It left an indelible impression on me.

All hairdressing money was deposited in the sugar bowl.

Whenever we needed to buy something—or needed money for school or anything like that—she opened the sugar bowl and made a "withdrawal."

Years later, she told me the sugar bowl never ran out of money while she was a widow. One way or another, there was always cash in there.

The sugar bowl never ran dry.

Sound familiar? It wasn't a continuous supply of flour or oil but a sugar bowl that never ran empty. Money doesn't grow on trees, but there was always enough in that sugar bowl. My mom and we kids experienced our very own "Widow of Zarephath" miracle.

God, My Father

God meets our needs. That's the conviction I was left with when I was a little boy. Whether through work He provided or the generosity of others, or through miracles, He was and is faithful.

One of the names of God in the Bible is "Jehovah Jireh," which means "The Lord Will Provide." Based on the experiences of my fatherless years, I concur. He is Jehovah Jireh to me.

He provided for our daily needs. I saw my mom put her trust in Him, and He came through. Time and again, we called on Him. Time and again, He heard our cries and answered. My dad was gone and couldn't provide for us anymore. Certain scriptures come to mind here. I see where God stepped in, and He showed Himself strong on our behalf (2 Chronicles 16:9). Also, He used his extraordinary riches in Christ Jesus to give us everything we needed (Philippians 4:19).

More than that, He became Father to me. I've always had a heavenly Father, and with hindsight, I can see how He made Himself known to me during these formative years. Spirit, soul, and body, He supplied all of our needs. I may not have fully recognized it as a young lad, but I see it now. Even if I couldn't fully appreciate it as a boy, my experience has formed a very thankful man.

Provision isn't always about meeting our physical or financial needs—although I don't discount those miracles. After all, God provides for the flowers of the field and the birds of the air (see Matthew 6:26–30). His revelation of Himself as my father had a much more significant impact on me. It is life to me. He became Father to me then, and He remains Father to me now.

The Gift of Community

I grew up attending a Christian Reformed Church. I am thankful for my faith heritage. I learned to value community and appreciate the spiritual gift of hospitality in my early years. It was demonstrated to me many times through the loving care of our church circle.

Whenever I read James 1:27, I'm reminded of how the church I grew up in met God's standard. In this passage, James wrote, "Religion that God our Father accepts as pure and faultless is this: to look after orphans and widows in their distress."

I almost got in trouble one day because my mom thought I hadn't listened to her instructions. We were headed out somewhere, and Mom asked me to ensure the screen door was closed. When we arrived back home, the door was propped open. Perturbed, she asked me why I hadn't listened. I thought I would get in big trouble, but it turns out I didn't. To my mom's surprise, the door was open because of the bags of groceries that someone had stuffed there. Some kind soul had left them there for our family.

My mom told me there were many times she was cleaning up after people had visited only to find money left under their coffee cups. I have memories of men from our church coming to repair a leaky roof; our freezer was always full of meat and vegetables. Our family and church community were generous beyond belief. Because of their gifts of food, money, and service, I can't remember experiencing lack or isolation. I love it when my mom reminds me of those beautiful gestures from caring people during our time of need.

There's one event, in particular, I remember.

The Gift of Christmas

Christmas has always been one of my favourite times of the year. Nowadays, it has come to mean a lot more, but in my childhood, it was mostly the stuff of dreams, lights, carols, and, of course, presents.

There was always a progression where Christmas was concerned. First, the lights were put up on the lampposts downtown. My mom loaded us into the car, and we headed downtown to see the lit-up bells, snowflakes, and Christmas tree at City Hall.

It was guaranteed that *The Sound of Music* would play on the television at that time of year. We got to watch most of it with my mom—but were always sent to bed with the Von Trapp children, "So long, farewell, *Auf Wiedersehen*, goodnight."

There was always the tree. It was a fake Tannenbaum, but the "magic" was real. There was a set pattern for putting up the Christmas tree in our home.

The evening's festivities started with a special dinner—something easy to clean up.

After supper, my mom put on "The Little Drummer Boy" by Don Janse and His Sixty Voice Children's Choir, our favourite Christmas record; and a hurried washing and drying of the dishes ensued. Once my sister, Debbie, and I were done, we quickly got into our pyjamas and rushed to the living room.

I can still remember the orderly way in which our Christmas tree was set up.

First came the base and the branches. After the tree was assembled, the lights were tested (fingers crossed that they all worked) and wrapped around the tree. Next came the shiny garland, and finally, my mom pulled out the beautiful glass ornaments.

After every ornament was hung correctly, the tree-topper came out. Ours was a white plastic star with lights. Finally, we were given an old milk bag full of last year's tinsel. My sister and I tossed it on the tree—and on each other—and the dancing and annual Christmas tree photoshoot began.

Of course, no tree is complete without gifts underneath it. We never lacked for anything, but this one year, there was precious little under the tree.

This can be distressing for a child. You have all the hopes and aspirations that come with Christmas. As I said, it was sort of magical to me. The Wish Book arrived in the mail, and dreaming, wishing, and hoping began. We saw the commercials on TV and dreamt of the latest and greatest toys. The Christmas songs only enhanced the experience with their talk of toys and Santa.

It seemed Christmas would be more of a dream than a reality. I was hoping for a Smash-Up Derby set (with "Buggem" and "Tough Tom"), but there was nothing under the tree close to the size of that toy. Christmas was approaching fast, and it looked like the dream would remain unfulfilled.

Then, one December evening, my mom got my sister and me ready for bed. As we went through the motions and routines, there was a knock at the front door. Mom told us to finish up while she went to the door. I remember her running back into the bathroom and telling us to come with her.

With no idea of what was going on, we followed her to the front door. What she showed us left an indelible mark on my heart and memory. The porch was covered with gifts, all neatly wrapped and stacked.

We stood there with our mouths open. It was like the scene in *Home Alone 2*, where the family wakes up to find their room full of gifts, all provided by Mr. Duncan. I can't get through that part of the movie without tearing up. I've lived it.

We were a "Christmas Eve" gift family. After an early dinner, we headed to the living room to open our gifts. Mom wanted to get us into bed early because we had to be up and ready for the candlelight service. I sang in the children's choir at our church and one of the featured events for the year was Christmas Eve.

There was great anticipation as we gathered around the tree, now surrounded by gifts. My mom wouldn't have known what presents were there because she hadn't wrapped them. One by one, we opened these beautiful gifts of generosity. I don't remember everything I received that year, but one present stands out in my memory.

I got Smash-Up Derby.

I believe God cares for and about us. He is Jehovah Jireh in the important things like being a Father to the fatherless or providing for our daily needs. He is also Jehovah Jireh in the seemingly unimportant things like a little boy and his Christmas wish for a Smash-Up Derby toy.

I'm not sure who left the gifts on our porch that night. I've asked my mom if she ever found or figured it out. She says she hasn't.

I know it wasn't Santa Claus. As much as my childlike imagination would have liked to go there, I knew it wasn't the case. This was a different kind of miracle.

It wasn't magic. The gifts didn't just appear after someone said, "Abracadabra!" They didn't materialize out of thin air. I knew someone had done this.

I believe it was a miracle of provision from a community of grace. Someone somewhere obeyed God and put my family's needs before their own. I believe it was our church community who showed up with a porch full of gifts. There was a strong precedent for it. They had done it over and over again.

Their generosity taught me that God, our Father, hears us and takes care of our needs. Their gift of love instilled the idea that God loves us through community. Their inexhaustible care for our family reinforced the foundation of hope we have in our steadfast Father.

I'll never forget.

I grew up in a church community that took what God said about Josiah in Jeremiah 22:16 seriously; "'He defended the cause of the poor and needy, and so all went well. Is that not what it means to know me?' declares the LORD."

Sure, it was hard for this little boy to grow up without his dad. But I experienced grace under pressure, acts of love from extended family and church community, and miracles of supply as my family was provided for. I never felt fatherless because I came to know who made me—who holds me—who knows me more than I know myself—who gives me all I need—and who loves me the most.

"Great is Thy faithfulness!"
"Great is Thy faithfulness!"
Morning by morning new mercies I see;

All I have needed Thy hand hath provided—
"Great is Thy faithfulness," Lord, unto me!
(Thomas O. Chisholm)

And I'm so thankful.

They say, "Hindsight is 20/20." As I look back on my fledgling years, I sure am glad that they were so formative. I couldn't know then what I know now, but the grace I experienced as a child would prepare me for the path ahead. And that path would prove to be tough as I moved from childhood to adulthood.

Chapter 2
NICU (Hope Realized)

By Your help, Your word I praise
I trust You, Lord, I'm not afraid
In You, I place my confidence
I do not hope in false pretense

Be brave, be strong
Do not give up
The Lord Himself
Will fill my cup
Be still, be quiet
Oh my soul
I place my trust in You, my Lord.
(Terry Posthumus, "By Your Help")

Paul, the apostle, connects the words *hope* and *expectation*. He does this in his letters to the Romans and the Philippians. In both cases, he adds "eager" to expectation (*see Romans 8:19 and Philippians 1:20*).

Eager expectation.

Hope.

As the father of many children, I can tell you a thing or two about expectation. All the dreams and hopes you have for your soon-to-arrive child. All that potential. You look forward to the hugs and kisses and the snuggle times. You dream about smiling and laughing together and even drying a few tears.

You never plan on a child coming too soon—or being born so sick they need life support.

When something like that happens, the dream becomes surreal. Anticipation becomes trepidation. And hope becomes a choice.

Lorraine

Lorraine and I met in Bible college.

I was the prototypical campus bad boy. Well, the prototypical Bible college campus bad boy. I wore Christian rock concert T-shirts. I listened to music way too loud. I talked too loudly and confronted those I perceived to have holier-than-thou attitudes.

Lorraine and I had some classes in common, and I found myself sitting next to her. A mutual friend had told me that she was offering haircuts for five bucks. Perfect for a student budget, and she was very pretty. I was smitten.

So I passed her a note. What swagger. Such confidence. I chuckle when I think about it today.

I asked her to cut my hair, and the flirtations commenced.

For me, it was pretty much love at first sight. For Lorraine, there was hesitation and doubt. And the day after she finally agreed to date me, she dropped a note in my mailbox. The note read, "I like you. But I think that this might be a mistake. I think we should just be friends."

How could she do this? The audacity. The unmitigated gall.

I was in love, so I threw caution to the wind. Mustering up some courage, I walked into the class that was about to begin and said, "Please come with me."

We walked to the student commons. I asked her to take a seat, and once she was comfortable, I took the note out of my pocket, threw it in her lap, and said, "This is BS. Last night, you said, 'yes' to me. You're going to try this, and you're going to like it."

She looked at the note, and then she looked at me. She said, "Okay."

I was astounded. I had been expecting a long and drawn-out conversation—maybe even some protest. But Lorraine said, "Okay."

We laughed about that so many times. But that was the beginning of Lorraine and me. From that point on, we were inseparable.

We both lived on campus and spent most of our waking hours together. It was a small bubble, and it wasn't the same as my previous dating experiences. We shared the same friends circle and class schedule. We ate, played, walked, talked, and prayed together. The environment was like dating in a pressure cooker. Not because there was a lot of pressure on us, but because it accelerated our relationship. For the good and not so good.

I had given Lorraine a promise ring for Christmas. In our minds, we were as good as engaged. After discussing our hopes and options moving forward, we decided that I should move to her hometown for the summer. We looked into jobs in the area, and I could secure an excellent job at a long-term care facility. The pay was great, and the opportunity was fantastic. Everything was looking up.

Problems arose as we spent so much time together. We were getting way too intimate. Lorraine and I spent too much time alone, and our defences crumbled—slowly, at first. But, the more we were together, the closer we wanted to be. Eventually, the situation spun out of control.

In July of 1986, Lorraine told me that she was pregnant less than a year after we met. Immediately, I went to the jeweller and bought her an engagement ring. Being practical, Lorraine told me to take it back because we couldn't afford it. Besides, she said, "I already have my ring," and assured me that it was enough.

We were afraid. But not of the pregnancy or the path that lay ahead. We worried about how this would impact our families and community. But we soldiered on and planned a wedding that would take place at the end of August.

My son, Theo, was born in January of 1987. We were just a couple of kids who were now raising a child. But we had each other, and we knew that we were in God's loving and protecting hands.

A year and a half later, our son Justin arrived on the scene.

In 1991, we were expecting yet another little one. Everything was progressing smoothly. Lorraine was a healthy young woman, and the baby was doing fine. So when she asked our family doctor whether it would be safe for her to travel twenty hours to her sister's wedding in Emo, Ontario, he said, "Yes."

Little did we know that something was going to go wrong. Terribly wrong.

Kara

My daughter, Kara, was born fourteen weeks premature. She weighed one pound nine ounces, and there were a lot of serious medical issues.

I have vivid memories of the night she arrived. I was at a business meeting when I received a long-distance emergency call. My brother-in-law told me that Lorraine had gone to the doctor because she wasn't feeling well. She had begun to develop extreme swelling in her feet, hands, and face.

Alarmed by what he saw, the doctor ordered an emergency medical evacuation. The caller said Lorraine was on her way to Toronto via air ambulance.

Imagine the shock. I felt isolated and helpless.

I immediately left for the hospital, waiting for Lorraine to arrive. What an agonizing couple of hours it was. Was my wife going to die? What about the baby? What was going to happen to the boys? How would I get them home?

After what seemed an interminable couple of hours, Lorraine's medivac arrived. When they brought her in, I had a difficult time recognizing her. It was immediately clear why the doctor had been so quick to act. Lorraine's face had swollen to what looked like twice its normal size.

The prognosis was that Lorraine was pre-eclamptic. Her life was at risk. The doctor said she would have to undergo an emergency C-section. He warned me the baby would not survive, as it would be fourteen weeks premature.

While this conversation was happening, Lorraine was being prepped for surgery. I heard her call for me from the hallway and went to be by her side.

The procedure began. I passed out—what a hero.

I came to at the moment Kara arrived. As the fog dissipated, I saw the staff running out of the room with a teeny-tiny baby. Everything was spinning. There was a frenetic buzz in the room as the doctors fought to save Lorraine's life. Yet a sense of peace settled into my heart. My memories are a blur from that evening. One thing seemed very clear to me. Lorraine and the baby would be all right.

After recovering from my fainting spell, Lorraine and I began to pray. We prayed for the baby. We prayed for the staff working on both her and the baby. We prayed for peace of heart and mind. And then we chuckled about the fainting knight in shining armour. It's funny, the things we remember.

All the while, the surgical staff kept going about their business. It was like we were in a bubble of peace amid frantic and urgent action.

While Lorraine was being stitched up, the doctor invited me to come and see our little girl. She was so small. Her entire body was the size of my right hand. I remember asking if I could touch her, and they said, "Yes. Please do. As often and as much as possible. She needs the connection." I was in awe that I could cover her with my hand.

When a child is born that early, there are many undeveloped things. Her eyes were still fused shut. There was no cartilage in her ears. Her skin was very thin and translucent. Her lungs had not yet developed the capacity to breathe air.

I didn't care about any of those things at that moment. The prognosis meant nothing to me. The voices around me became distant and muted as I stood there, holding my little girl. I knew she would make it. Don't ask me how I knew. The simplest way to describe it would be to say I knew it in my heart.

Visiting Lorraine and Kara was challenging because I also had the two little lads to care for. By now, the boys had arrived home. They had travelled back with Lorraine's sister. But Lorraine was still in the hospital recovering. The doctors were trying to figure out what was going on with her. They ran test after test to determine what had caused her body to react the way it did.

I had to continue working throughout this ordeal. We still had to make rent, pay the utility bills, and put food on the table. At the time, we did not have extra money. Every month was a financial challenge. Now I had to find a way to pay for sitters, the extra fuel it took to drive back and forth, and parking.

My visits to the hospital consisted of me going from Lorraine to Kara and back again. I went from ward to ward. We learned Lorraine had a condition called thrombocytosis. But in the early days, we had no idea how or why the pre-eclampsia had happened. It was difficult to watch my wife go through this trial. She was undergoing a constant barrage of tests, and some of them were very painful. One time, when it seemed Lorraine was going to break, I got into a verbal altercation with a lab tech. They had come to take yet another blood sample, and Lorraine needed a break.

This was a very stressful time for us.

Over the coming hours and days, we began to understand the difficulty of the journey ahead. Kara had survived the stress and shock of her early arrival. But so many things could still go wrong as she developed outside of the womb.

One issue that quickly became a factor was her little heart.

To gain access to the NICU, I had to dress like a surgeon. First, I washed my hands with surgical-grade soap and put on a surgeon's gown. I had to wear a mask to ensure I would not introduce any virus to the ward. It was all planned and staged with great care. Every time I visited, I went through the same ritual.

Once prepped, I signed in to the ward and waited for an update on Kara's status.

Day after day, I sat vigil by her incubator.

Life and death waged war moment to moment there in the NICU. We experienced minor victories and miracles in the early days after Kara was born. She lost weight and measured less than a pound. She was also on high oxygen levels as she fought for every breath.

At times, the frenetic NICU was the only peaceful place in my life. Funny how that works. I would sit with Kara for a few hours, listening to Michael Card's "Sleep Sound in Jesus." We had that tape playing on a continuous loop throughout Kara's stay at Mount Sinai.

I remember the day I was told about the holes in Kara's heart. After performing the prep ritual, I went into the NICU only to discover a team had been working on Kara. The doctor on duty noticed me approaching and came to intercept me.

He told me Kara was not responding to her treatments. Kara's blood-oxygen levels were not normal, and this was a cause for concern. He then told me they had performed an ultrasound on Kara and discovered three holes in her heart.

The doctor gave me two options to mull over. Both sounded (and really were) very bad. He said they could treat Kara with steroids to encourage development. The other option was open-heart surgery to repair the holes.

Steroids? Open heart surgery? The idea of either option seemed ludicrous to me. She was tiny, and she seemed to be getting smaller. I wondered how these things could even be possible.

As I stood there in stunned silence, the doctor told me both treatments were very risky. He then put his hand on my shoulder and told me I should prepare to say goodbye to Kara.

Goodbye? Oh, God, no.

Somehow, I mustered the courage to tell the doctor I needed to pray about this. I then pushed past him and headed to Kara's incubator.

As I sat there, wondering what to do, I heard someone say to me, "Lay your hands on her. And pray." I turned to see who it was, but there was nobody there.

Cue the goosebumps.

I thought, *Great. Now I'm losing my mind. I've snapped under pressure.*

But the voice that had spoken to me seemed so real. So I asked the age-old question used by children everywhere. "Huh?"

And I heard again, "Lay your hands on her. And pray."

I did.

I reached into her incubator and placed my hand on Kara. I prayed, "Lord, I don't know where to find it in the Bible, but I know it's there. You work through the act of laying on of hands and praying. Please heal my little girl."

And that was it.

Nothing happened at that moment. No light. No heat. Not even a "warm and fuzzy" feeling.

So I pulled my hand out of the incubator and closed the little round door.

At the time, we lived far away from the hospital. This meant I couldn't visit every single day. I wanted to stay with Lorraine and Kara 24/7, but it wasn't possible. I waited until the last possible moment, and I made the long drive home.

The time between visits was excruciating. Hours felt like days, and days felt like weeks.

After what seemed like an eternity, I returned to the hospital. I washed, put on my scrubs and mask, and headed into the NICU.

Déjà vu.

As I walked toward Kara's incubator, there was a team packing up some medical equipment. The doctor noticed me approaching and came over to intercept.

He told me the team had done another ultrasound on Kara. He told me they could not find the holes that were there before. He said they couldn't find a single hole in Kara's heart.

And then he said, "Whatever you're doing, keep doing it."

Cue hope.

There were many more stories of small victories during Kara's fledgling days. By Christmas, she had progressed to the point she could transfer to Level 2.

Then came the day our baby girl finally came home with us.

Thinking back on those days fills me with a sense of awe. I still marvel at how this little preemie girl had come through. With the holes in her heart, this one-pound nine-ounce baby survived. And this once-voiceless child filled our home with cries and giggles and "I love you, Daddy!"s.

Today, Kara is a healthy, happy, and vibrant woman. She is an incredible artist. And get this, the preemie was the first of my children to make me a grandfather.

Hope realized.

Once, on my way home from work, a pickup truck took a ninety-degree turn across five lanes of traffic. It didn't seem possible, but there it was. Unexpected. Sudden. Violent.

Sometimes life does that.

Sometimes we get blindsided even when we think we have our eyes wide open.

Sometimes life "turns on a dime"—when you least expect it. And you're left standing there wondering, "How could this have happened?"

Chapter 3
I Am Not My Own

Q. What is your only comfort in life and in death?
A. That I am not my own, but belong—body and soul, in life
and in death—to my faithful Saviour, Jesus Christ.
(Heidelberg Catechism, Q&A 1)

I'm looking forward to meeting my daughters, Gracie and Cherie. It shocks most people when I tell them how many children I have. I guess it helps them to remember who I am. "You're the guy with eleven kids." No matter what I've done or where I've been, when I am introduced to someone new, "and he's got, eleven kids … Can you believe that?" makes its way into the conversation.

I love it!

You'd have to love kids to have this many.

The truth is, I have more. Fourteen, to be exact.

Gracie

I'm not covering much of Gracie's story in this book. Not that losing her wasn't grievous for Lorraine and me. The loss of a child is devastating. It leaves you feeling empty. You struggle with self-imposed accusations, doubts, and fears. You wonder if you'll be able to carry on.

Although I'm only covering Gracie's story briefly, I'm not glossing it over. She's not a byline in our story. As Lorraine carried her for a few short months, the time that we had Gracie left a profound impact on our lives.

Gracie died as a result of an early-term miscarriage. She was so small. We couldn't be sure of the gender, but Lorraine was sure she had been carrying a girl.

It all happened so quickly.

Lorraine called me at work. I dropped everything and drove home at breakneck speed. I was in shock and very worried.

When I arrived home, Lorraine was sitting on the deck. In her hand, she held a heart-shaped tin box. In that box was Gracie's teeny-tiny body.

I held Lorraine as we cried together, grieving the loss of this precious little one. Then she told me what she wanted to do. I grabbed her by the shoulders, looked into her eyes, and nodded.

We cried some more and reached out for the comfort only God, our Father, could give.

Lorraine requested that we go and find a quiet place with a big old tree. She wanted to bury the little heart-shaped box.

We drove around town, found the perfect spot, and buried our daughter, Gracie. I had my guitar, and we sang a couple of our favourite worship songs. Then we prayed as we surrendered our little girl to the One who loves us the most. After that, we sat in silence and waited for a peaceful release.

A short amount of time had passed when I looked at Lorraine, and she nodded. It was time to walk away.

And as we walked away, Lorraine looked at me and said, "It's going to be okay."

And at that moment, I knew she was right.

We were at peace and knew that we would get through this. There would be tough days, to be sure. But we were okay. We were safe. Gracie was safe.

And slowly, we began to heal.

Cherie

July 2003 was a month marked by crisis. SARS had taken a toll in Toronto, and the city was slumping. So much so, SARStock, a benefit concert organized by the Rolling Stones and featuring Canadian and international artists, had been planned.

The concert was scheduled for July 30. It would be amazing, and I was so excited to watch it on TV.

But I never got the chance.

After I arrived home from work on the evening of the twenty-ninth, I noticed Lorraine did not look well. Her complexion had taken on a greyish tone, and she complained of having pains in her abdomen.

I leapt into action.

After calling the birthing suite at the hospital, we rushed over. Lorraine was about eight and a half months pregnant at the time.

It shouldn't have been a problem. We had done the early arrival thing before. *Two weeks?* I thought. *Bring it on!*

Lorraine was immediately connected to a fetal heart monitor when we got to the hospital. The machine has a very distinct sound. It's comforting to hear the little heart beating. I had heard it many times before. It sounds like the heart is declaring, "Wow! Wow! Wow!"

It was alarming when I didn't hear that sound. I recalled having heard even the faintest of heartbeats. Hoping against hope, I exclaimed, "There it is!" But the nurse kept moving the sensor around. The pulse was Lorraine's, not Cherie's, and the room took on an atmosphere of quiet desperation.

Out of nowhere, the machine leapt to life as Lorraine went into labour. It showed strong contractions, but there was still no pulse.

No matter, I thought. The baby will be here in a few minutes. Then the doctors will be able to help both of them.

Things progressed quickly, and Lorraine delivered what looked like a perfect little girl. But the baby wasn't making any sound. There were none of the usual signs that accompanied the arrival of a newborn.

The doctor cut the umbilical cord and rushed her to the warmer. There, the team tried to rouse Cherie, clearing her airway—trying to stimulate her breathing.

No response. No movement.

I cried out in prayer and went to where they were working on Cherie. The atmosphere was tense. The doctors and nurses continued all the routines. They kept trying to get her to cry.

Nothing.

Time for a different tactic.

The doctor put a breathing mask on her.

Then he began to perform CPR.

Next, he injected her with adrenaline.

The doctor tried everything. No option or expense was held back. The team worked on Cherie for what felt like an eternity.

I called out to God, "Please, let my little girl cry." Crying babies are breathing babies. Breathing babies are living babies.

"Let her live!"

The doctor did everything he could. And with no other options available, he looked at me and said, "There's nothing else I can do. I'm so sorry."

I stood there, stunned. The world was spinning and silent. I couldn't believe this was happening. How could this have transpired? What was going on here? I was in shock.

As I began to regain my bearings, I heard Lorraine wailing. She was crying out to the doctors, asking them to keep going. All the while, she had been attended to because she had gone through the delivery of a baby.

It was surreal to go through all the things people go through when a baby is delivered. The contractions. The encouragement. The hopeful anticipation. Only we were empty-handed. No baby. All the promise and potential deflated.

We weren't ready to give up the fight. I couldn't accept the doctor's words. After all, God had healed my daughter, Kara, when she had nothing going for her. The same God could raise my daughter, Cherie. He would have to because I was not going to give up. I wouldn't let go, and I would assail heaven's gates until He gave me what I wanted.

And that's what we did. I held my daughter in my arms, and we began to plead, bargain, and fight for our girl.

Through the night and early into the following day, Lorraine and I prayed over Cherie. We proclaimed our faith to our loving and faithful God. We reminded Him of the promises we had stood upon ... promises from His Word. We used our words to pray to God, and when words failed, we groaned our petitions. I sang over her. We asked the Holy Spirit to pray on our behalf. We wept—caught our breath—and then started again.

Every promise. Every thread of hope we could find in the Scriptures and muster within ourselves. We pulled out all the stops in desperate hope. We fought in faith to utter exhaustion.

As we prayed, I was holding the body of my little girl. She had dark hair and tiny, delicate lips. She was so beautiful. Her tiny fingers, though cold, were perfect. In my mind, it would be so easy for God to breathe the breath of life into her. Then she would live. Cherie would open her eyes, and I would love her with all the love a father can give.

So why not, Lord? What's the problem here? What am I doing wrong?

My prayers began to turn to complaints, disappointment, and rage. I didn't understand. This didn't compute. It wasn't fair, and I wanted my daughter back. Failing that, God had better give me some answers.

That's how I was beginning to feel.

I have a good memory, and I have high expectations of God. I believed His Word, and I took Him at His promises. If He had healed Kara when there was no earthly hope for her, why wouldn't He raise Cherie? Was it our sin? Had we failed God? Were we being punished for something?

Of course not.

But I still sought answers. The whole thing wasn't right, and I didn't believe God operated the way things were playing out. I remembered the story of Elijah raising the son of the Widow of Zarephath from the dead (1 Kings 17:21–22). Jesus did it several times in scripture. Lazarus (John 11:38–44). The Widow of Nain's son (Luke 7:11–17).

Why not now? Why not Cherie? Why not me?

I had to get out of the hospital for a little while. The walls were starting to close in on me, and my raging against whatever wasn't helping matters. Lorraine had fallen asleep, and I left her to rest. I wanted to go home to tell the kids what had and hadn't happened and figure out what was going on.

I needed answers, and I wasn't having much luck getting them by myself. The reality was that I was getting further from the truth. I was losing perspective and footing. My angst was beginning to take me to some pretty dark places. I was getting very angry with God, and I felt betrayed and victimized. I also started looking for reasons it had happened. I was looking for something—or someone—to blame. I was caustic and spiralling out of control. I knew this was not good, and I needed to do something about it.

The only thing I could think to do was reach out to my friend Harry. He had been a fatherlike mentor to me in the years before this tragedy. I didn't seem to be getting answers from God—not that I was giving much time to trying to hear—so I reached out to Harry. His was a voice of reason, calm, and assurance in my oft-turbulent life.

The problem was, he wasn't home when I called.

But his wife Erika was. She had been as influential in my life as Harry had. They were the actual package deal. Not only that, but she also always fed me when I visited. There are still days I crave her delicious cream puffs. Erika was a voice of encouragement to me. She was the one who challenged and cheered me as I transitioned from trying to be a "rock star" into a worship leader. From a leadership standpoint, she was the one who gave me the platform. That encouragement launched my music ministry.

I told Erika I needed to speak with Harry, and she asked me what was going on.

I told her about what had happened and how I didn't understand it. With great wisdom, Erika asked me to tell her what I meant.

I told her about Kara's story and how God had healed her heart.

I said, "Why won't God give Cherie back? He healed Kara when she had the holes in her heart."

Erika must have sensed the Spirit leading her because she asked me a critical question.

"What happened when Kara was healed?"

So I told her, "God told me to lay my hands on her."

"Stop," she said. "What's God saying to you right now?"

"Let her go." I knew it, and I didn't want that.

I wasn't ready to say it out loud.

When I didn't respond to her, Erika said, "You know, Terry, you have to listen to what God is telling you in every situation."

"I don't want that."

She said, "I know."

I thanked Erika for talking with me and hung up the phone. I had my answer, only I was not ready to accept it.

One of the things to be done that day was to make the necessary arrangements for Cherie's interment. That was surreal. I never thought I would have to buy a coffin and grave plot for my child. Add to that the fact there is a "commercial" aspect to interments. I felt I was being upsold at every turn. It left me feeling jaded and tired.

When I was done arranging Cherie's funeral and burial, I headed back to the hospital. When I arrived, I found Lorraine holding Cherie and praying God would give her back. She looked so broken and lost. I took Cherie from her arms and held Lorraine while she wept and questioned and wept some more. She told me we were not going to give up. Lorraine had all the faith needed, and she was tenacious.

Lorraine told me she needed to rest and asked me to keep on praying. So I took Cherie in my arms, sat in the rocking chair, and began to cry out to God. I knew what He had told me when I was speaking with Erika. I hadn't been ready to tell Lorraine about the conversation yet. I wasn't even prepared to accept it myself at that point. I was broken-hearted.

If I had a bucket, I would've filled it with tears. I cried until there were no tears left, and then I cried some more. The tears began to flow while I held Cherie, singing lullabies to her.

My eyes burned. My heart ached. My mind raced.

During this time, I accepted what God said to me when Erika asked me what He was saying. "Let her go."

Empty and broken, I muttered through gritted teeth, "Fine. You can have her."

He whispered, "She was always mine … and so are you, Lorraine, and all your children. I've got this. I've got you."

I began to surrender.

He said, "Cherie was not born to you. She was 'borne' into glory—into My arms. And I will give you a pound of joy for every ounce of sorrow."

I broke down—and let all doubt and rage go. It was good to take a moment of rest in the arms of my Father. The One who made me. The One who knows me best. The One who loves me the most.

Gathering myself, I rose from the rocking chair and walked over to Lorraine. She turned her head to watch my approach, and as she looked into my eyes, she began to shake her head.

"No. No. We have to keep fighting," she cried.

I said, "We have to let her go."

"No," she replied.

I knew what she was going through. I felt what she was feeling. The pain was too much to bear. It didn't seem right.

But I put Cherie in the bed the hospital had provided and took Lorraine in my arms. I began to pray—and after a while, she joined me.

As we prayed, we began to release our desires to God. We asked Him to comfort our pain and to give us peace. This had been a tough decision for us. We asked God to forgive us and to reassure us. We asked Him to help us understand and to make the impossible possible.

I told Lorraine about my conversation with Erika. I explained how God had spoken. How we were to "let her go." I hoped she understood the way I had. And I prayed she would be able to find peace in this storm. I also told her about my conversation with God while sitting in the rocking chair—how He would give us a pound of joy for every ounce of sorrow.

While we were praying, something strange happened to me. I had a vision.

I'm not the kind of person that "gets" visions regularly. Also, I've been manipulated by people who prophesied "visions" over me. When you start attributing "Thus sayeth the Lord" to your dreams, there are many risks.

This was different, though. I knew God was speaking to us. It's like the few times I have heard God speak in an audible voice. In those cases, it was life or death.

In my vision, I saw Lorraine walking down a beach. She was holding the hand of a little boy in one hand and a little girl in the other.

That was it. That was the entirety of my vision.

In 2005, our twins arrived. A little girl and a little boy.

Such joy. A pound of joy for every ounce of sorrow.

The vision wasn't complicated, and it wasn't long. There was no room for interpretation. Couple it with the promise, though, and I'm still blown away to this day. God cares for us, and He is faithful to His promises.

There's a risk in telling a story like this. The point could be misconstrued. I don't want you to think the message is that God replaced Cherie with the twins. Nothing could be further from the truth.

I heard God say that He would give us a pound of joy for every ounce of sorrow. He did replace something, but it was not Cherie. It was sorrow. And it was traded for joy.

This leads me to the final part of this story.

From what I understand, most people don't have funerals after a stillbirth. We did, and it was a beautiful celebration of life. For me, few moments compare. It was a time when our community surrounded us, holding us and giving us the strength and courage to go on. It was one of the moments when I felt God's love through others. Both present and past, our church families showed up en masse, and there was standing room only.

We felt their love, their support, and their prayers. They wept with us as we grieved our stillborn daughter. They held us tight so we would not falter. They stood in the gap and took care of our needs.

It gave me hope.

The Bible verse I chose for the service comes from Romans 15:13. It reads: "May the God of hope fill you with all joy and peace as you trust in him, so that you may overflow with hope by the power of the Holy Spirit."

My friends David and Deborah joined me in song as we led all those gathered at the funeral. We sang "Trading My Sorrows" with one voice. All those in attendance surrounded Lorraine, the children, and me with compassion. As we stood at Cherie's graveside, we were not alone. Many hands shared the load as I placed Cherie's tiny white coffin in the ground. The heart of our community broke with ours, and together, we healed.

The grief of losing Cherie weighed on us for months. Her stillbirth took a toll on us, and we had a hard time moving past it. It felt like we were bogged down. We were spinning our wheels.

Lorraine struggled with guilt, and it was hard to see my wife suffering like that. I knew she was blaming herself for our daughter's death.

Being so low was out of character for Lorraine. She was a strong woman of faith. She was known for encouraging others in their faith. She always reminded anyone who listened to "speak words of life." Lorraine was one of those people who truly lived out their faith.

In truth, I owe Lorraine a debt of gratitude. I would not be the man of faith I am today without her impact and influence on my life. She challenged my thoughts, words, and motivations early in our relationship and our married years.

You can understand my concern when Lorraine seemed to be crashing and burning. It was inconsistent with who she was to the kids and me.

Lorraine began questioning everything that had happened during the pregnancy. She replayed the events of the day that led up to the tragedy. It was one step forward, two steps back, and it was not a good situation.

With skewed retrospect, Lorraine began questioning the medical decisions. This included not just the decisions made on the evening of Cherie's stillbirth but also those made by our doctor throughout the pregnancy. There had been some minor concerns during Lorraine's third trimester that hadn't alarmed the doctors. But in hindsight, this all came into question. Every doctor visit, every conversation, every prognosis fell under the microscope.

I tried to assure Lorraine she had done nothing wrong. I wanted to encourage her to move away from a self-destructive line of thinking. Wave after wave of sorrow kept overcoming her, sending her plummeting into despair.

I grew afraid for my wife. I felt useless. It seemed like there was nothing I could do to help her.

Again, I found myself crying out to God for help. Lorraine was grief-stricken and tired. It seemed she didn't have the strength to help herself.

Our home was slowly becoming a toxic environment. Lorraine didn't want it to be that way, but her pain was causing her to become caustic toward herself, her faith, and life in general. It was beginning to affect everything, and I was scared.

One Saturday morning, a few months after Cherie's death, I sat Lorraine down in the quiet privacy of our bedroom. We needed to talk things out, and we needed to pray.

I started by telling Lorraine how I loved her and always would. We had been through many things together, and this wasn't going to tear us apart.

I told her that Cherie's death was not her fault. She rejected this outright.

I pushed on. I told her that the doctor had pulled me aside to tell me there was nothing that could have been done. He said that had he been standing ready, scalpel in hand, he wouldn't have been able to save Cherie.

He wanted to assure us of two things. First, that the whole thing had been entirely out of our hands. There was nothing she had done to cause it. There was nothing we could have done to prevent it.

Second, he wanted to assure me Cherie didn't suffer. According to the doctor, death is immediate when the placenta separates from the uterus. He said that even if he knew the exact moment it happened, not even an emergency C-section would have been fast enough.

None of this mattered to Lorraine.

Pressing on, I reminded her of God's promises to us. They had come to us immediately after we surrendered our will concerning Cherie to God. He had promised us Cherie had been "borne into His arms," and He would give us "a pound of joy for every ounce of sorrow."

At that moment, Lorraine didn't want promises. I understood. We wanted our daughter. Barring that, we wanted answers.

Lorraine needed a breakthrough, the kind only God could give.

As she sat there crying, I took her face into my hands and told her she had been a faithful mom to Cherie throughout the pregnancy. I wanted her to know she had done everything she could in the days leading to Cherie's delivery. I tried to reassure her that I believed in her and did not blame her for this.

Over and over, I told her these things. Each time, she rejected them. I was beginning to think I was going to lose her. I wasn't sure we were going to make it through this storm.

It was then that the Parable of the Talents popped into my mind. In particular, I remembered the words of the master who said, "Well done, good and faithful servant!" Those words resonated deep within my soul, and I knew I had to share them with Lorraine.

When I did, something shifted in the conversation. Something flickered to life in Lorraine's eyes, and she asked me to repeat what I had just said.

I grabbed my Bible and opened it to Matthew 25 and read from verse 21: "Well done, good and faithful servant! You have been faithful with a few things; I will put you in charge of many things. Come and share your master's happiness."

As soon as I finished reading the Scripture passage, Lorraine said, "You're right." I was so happy to hear her say that.

I said, "You were faithful when you carried and cared for Cherie. You took care of yourself. You ate healthy foods and rested as much as you needed. When you had to visit the doctor, you went. No complaints. You followed their advice.

"More than that, you prayed over Cherie. You played worship music for her, and you spoke words of truth and life to her."

I continued, "God knows. He saw it all, and He is pleased with you. You were loyal with small things. He will let you care over great things. He will share His joy with you. He will give you a pound of joy for every ounce of sorrow."

The process of healing began on that day. Lorraine often referred to that conversation as the turning point in her grief after Cherie's death.

I'm so thankful that the Spirit reminded us of the Parable of the Talents on that day. When I tried to reassure Lorraine, the words seemed hollow. But when God spoke to us through His Word, the message was full of life and grace. His words gave us footing on a slippery slope. The Word of God gave us something to grab on to when we found ourselves falling. His Word was and is the truth (John 17:17) and gives life (John 6:63).

Losing a child is one of the hardest things a person can go through. A part of you dies too. Grief and guilt are ruthless foes that can trip you up and suffocate even the strongest of us.

But God has given us gifts to combat the pain, sorrow, and loss. He has given us hope through His promises and through community. The first part of Romans 8:28 says, "We know that in all things God works for the good of those who love him."

Those words got "stuck in my craw." I almost choked on them. Hearing someone offhandedly repeat that Scripture brought a visceral response rooted in pain and grief.

And yet, I know today that these words are right. It has nothing to do with hindsight. It has to do with the deeply rooted truth integral in God's Word. These words are the truth. They always have been, and they don't stop being true because we suffer. Even repeated by well-meaning but ignorant people, the words in Romans 8:28 are authentic, accurate, and genuine.

I started the chapter with a quote from the Heidelberg Catechism. I studied it as a young man. It was part of my journey as I matured into Christian adulthood. Am I ever glad I did.

I know that I am not my own.

For that matter, my wife and my children are also not my own.

I know that we belong, body and soul, in life and death, to our faithful Saviour, Jesus Christ.

Chapter 4
NICU (Hope Deferred)

You made all the delicate, inner parts of my body
and knit me together in my mother's womb.
Thank you for making me so wonderfully complex!
Your workmanship is marvellous—how well I know it.
You watched me as I was being formed in utter seclusion,
as I was woven together in the dark of the womb.
You saw me before I was born.
Every day of my life was recorded in your book.
Every moment was laid out
before a single day had passed. (Psalm 139:13–16 NLT)

I spent sixteen days in the NICU with my son, Ezekiel. I'll get to that later because his medical journey began in utero. And, oh, what a ride that was! It was fast and furious.

The story began when Lorraine and I went in for a routine prenatal checkup. During the visit, our doctor noticed an alarming issue. Ezekiel was accumulating an abnormal amount of fluid in his chest cavity. And this was serious because his organs were free-floating in his chest.

This diagnosis prompted an emergency procedure. The surgery took place while Ezekiel was in utero—still in the womb. And Lorraine came home the same day as the surgery. It was amazing and alarming, and I am still in awe thinking about it.

The procedure was successful, but this was the beginning of a challenging trial for our family. Ezekiel underwent a series of tests that got to the underlying cause of the fluid buildup. Echocardiograms. Ultrasounds. Genetic tests. Over the coming weeks, we visited one clinic or another, two to three times a week.

I found a letter I had written to our friends and family. It's incredible how hope rings true through the words we shared. I would say we were encouraging others, and through it, we got encouraged.

Here's an excerpt:

Continue to pray for Lorraine, Ezekiel and me. We are praying that the baby will go full-term and that he will be able to come home with us and live a full and vibrant life. We are also praying that the condition that caused this will be wholly rectified and set straight.

God is good, and He has once again taught us that He knows the beginning from the end. We thank God for His provision and the guidance He gives when we seek after Him. He never leaves us or forsakes us. We thank God for the doctor and his team and the wisdom and knowledge that steadied us throughout this process. We also thank God for everyone who has lifted this before God in prayer.

What a blessing! What support! We are so thankful!

One of the tests Ezekiel needed was an echocardiogram.

I hate sitting in waiting rooms. I've been there many times. Too many times.

With that in mind, we arrived at the appointment with plenty of time to spare. And then we waited for two hours. I did not need the extra stress. The situation could have proven to be quite volatile.

But God had something else in mind for us. His scope is much broader than ours. He knew who was going to be there on that particular day. He knew the stories and needs. Instead of letting us languish, He allowed us to offer encouragement to someone who needed it.

A young couple was waiting in the room with us. They were pretty concerned about their soon-to-arrive baby, who had a potential heart murmur.

God knew what they needed and allowed us to step into their world for a few brief moments.

Choosing hope usually means acknowledging your feelings and surrendering them. In this case, we decided to abandon our feelings of frustration and fear. In doing so, we spent the entire two hours encouraging this young couple. When they were in the echocardiogram clinic, we continued to pray for them and their child.

Thinking back on this, I would say our encouragement for that day came from us extending the same. This couple had a desperate need. We responded and were able to be a voice of hope.

Later that day, we happened to cross paths with the same couple. We had no plans to reconnect, but God had His idea. It's funny how these little divine appointments work out. It turns out we would be the ones who needed a bit of encouragement later that day. And we got encouraged when this couple happened upon us in one of the busier parts of Toronto.

With great excitement and relief, they told us their baby was fine. We were so happy for them. And we walked away with our hope renewed as we thanked God for hearing our prayers.

Ezekiel was born on December 6, 2006. We had learned he had Down syndrome a couple of weeks prior. We knew there were significant challenges Ezekiel was facing. We were on high alert because the doctor had told us he would likely be premature. We had no idea of the flurry and fury with which he would enter our lives.

During one of our "routine" visits (nothing much was routine in those days), it was discovered that Ezekiel had removed one of the shunts that had been used to relieve the pressure created by the extra fluids in his chest and abdomen. The doctor suggested that we try again because the shunts had been producing good results up to that point.

The risk was that the procedure might put Lorraine into labour because her water could be broken during the operation. We prayed about it and agreed that he should proceed with the procedure. Our doctor wanted to do it that very day.

So we headed off to Mount Sinai Hospital, a place all too familiar to Lorraine and me. We met with a pediatric specialist who informed us of the pitfalls associated with Down syndrome and hydrops. Knowing this, we felt we learned how to pray for Ezekiel and those providing his care.

As Lorraine was being prepped for surgery, Ezekiel took a turn for the worse. The fetal heart monitor indicated that his heart rate had plummeted. We knew that this sometimes happened during ultrasounds.

Typically, doctors roll the mom on her side to ease the problem. Usually, the baby's heart rate increases again. That was not the case.

It was some of the most organized and lucid chaos I have ever seen. I was amazed at how calm and decisive the doctors and staff were as they moved Lorraine from the procedure room to labour and delivery, into a room where they confirmed that Zee's heart rate was still dangerously low, and then into the operating room.

Ezekiel came into this world via an emergency C-section. He was born without a heartbeat, and the medical staff whisked him away. As I stood there in shock, with my wife getting the medical attention she needed, the doctor approached me. He wanted to know "how far to take this."

Cue hope.

I told the doctor to do everything they could, and God would lead them. He said, "Okay," and left me to pray. Darkness tried to suffocate me, but the light of hope kept on shining. In that situation, I was not about to let it go.

I stood in the hallway outside the operating room for seven minutes (which, I must admit, felt like hours). And then, the door burst open, and the doctor took me to see my newborn son, Ezekiel.

Anticipating Ezekiel's arrival, we resisted pinning our expectations on percentages and prognoses. Our hope was in the Lord. And the events of the next fifteen days presented many challenges to our faith. Edema. Non-functioning kidneys. These were two of the many medical challenges Ezekiel faced.

We found out he had pulmonary hypertension in the days after his birth. The artery between his heart and lungs was not large enough. This means the heart must work harder to get blood to the lungs. And this leads to the heart becoming enlarged and weakened.

The doctors were very clear with us about their prognosis for Ezekiel. They were doing everything they could to help him, but they did not expect him to survive.

That's hard to hear. We wanted our son to be well.

During Ezekiel's stay in the NICU, he underwent several treatments and procedures. His biggest challenge was that he could not breathe on his own. The doctor put him on a respirator to help him breathe. They used every means at their disposal, including new and hybrid techniques.

I visited Lorraine and Ezekiel every day. And every day, I got a mix of good and not-so-good news. On the one hand, Ezekiel's kidneys started to function. On the other, his heart had become enlarged. At the same time, the doctor informed us that his blood oxygen levels were too low.

It was a constant tug-of-war between encouraging and discouraging news. The doctors, engaged in a tough fight to save Ezekiel's life, were fighting a losing battle. Time and options were running out.

On December 19, 2006, I received a call from the NICU. The doctor in charge of Ezekiel's treatment asked to meet with us. The staff at Mount Sinai had done everything they could. They consulted with the team at SickKids hospital. They were also out of options.

The doctor told us Ezekiel was succumbing to pulmonary hypertension. Hydrops complicated the matter. Ezekiel had become unresponsive. The oxygen saturation in his blood was too low, despite the fact he was on 100 percent oxygen.

The only option left was for the doctor to paralyze Ezekiel. This meant a machine would have to take over his breathing completely.

His recommendation was the removal of the ventilation machine. The doctor held little hope Ezekiel would survive, with or without it. Lorraine and I felt life support was not a good option. We didn't want to put our son through that. It wouldn't be fair to him.

Ezekiel needed a miracle. We clung to hope. We prayed he would be able to breathe on his own.

The doctors had run out of options, but we hadn't. Hope is not tied to circumstances. We had never pinned our hopes on medical reports.

Our only option came from resting in Christ and His presence. This hadn't changed before, and it wouldn't change now. Our hope remained. To quote that good old hymn,

My hope is built on nothing less,
Than Jesus' blood and righteousness ...

When every earthly prop gives way,
He then is all my Hope and Stay.

With that hope, Lorraine and I, along with a few close friends, gathered together to pray. After that, we went to Ezekiel's incubator and waited as the doctor removed the breathing tube.

After the tube was removed, I heard Ezekiel's voice for the first and only time. He cried out, and Lorraine and I wept at the sound of it. I will never forget that beautiful little yelp. It lingers in my heart and mind, and I no longer remember the sounds of the NICU.

Moments later, Ezekiel fell silent. Thirty minutes later, he died. I held my little boy as he passed from this life into the arms of Jesus. This event became imprinted on my heart and soul. The ecstasy of victory and the pain of loss will do that.

I had loved Ezekiel as I love all my children. I was shattered. I had hoped that God would heal him with all my heart, and I held on to that hope until the very end.

We left the hospital broken and empty-handed. Hope faltered and faded out.

I felt numb as well-meaning friends took us for dinner. Their voices, a buzz. Their well-wishes fell on deaf ears.

I couldn't believe that this had happened again.

Cue despair.

I remember the feelings of darkness and brokenness as I placed his coffin in the ground. I felt angry. I felt betrayed.

We had held on to God throughout. We were testifying of His goodness and grace. We stood in faith, utterly dependent on God. We boldly proclaimed the truths of His Word and encouraged others wherever possible. We hadn't wavered and taken our eyes off God. We had kept the faith.

Once again, I thought about the miracle of Kara. If God could heal her, why didn't He heal Ezekiel? I felt ripped off.

I was ready, willing, and able to raise a boy with Down syndrome. I was prepared for the challenges we might face along the way. I was not afraid of what a life with my son, Ezekiel, was or wasn't going to be.

We buried Ezekiel on December 22, right next to his sister, Cherie. Surrounded by friends and family, I placed the tiny white coffin in the ground.

That day, the grave almost swallowed my soul. This was the darkest of days. I couldn't believe that we were here again. The foundation beneath me gave way. My perspective shifted, and I began to slide. The darkness closed in on me, and I couldn't see a way out. The light of hope flickered and waned.

I thought of Gracie and Cherie, and I thought, "Are You kidding me? What's enough? How much more do You want to take? How could You let this happen?"

If not for the loving and supportive hands of friends, family, and a caring community, I would not have made it. They held me up, literally and figuratively. They stood with us at the grave and walked with us in the following days. They showed us God's love.

What about God? How did He respond?

He didn't pull away. He didn't leave or forsake me. He didn't change his opinion of me. In fact, with hindsight, I can tell you I know He was with me the entire time. He didn't become offended by my bluster. He didn't write me off. He didn't "you of little faith" me.

Quite the opposite.

God comforted me as He waited with me. His heart broke with mine because He understood my pain. He shepherded me through the "valley of the shadow of death."

I grieved and healed over the days and weeks that followed Ezekiel's departure. After a time, the flame of hope would begin to flicker back to life.

Time and Again

It's incredible that God can use something simple, obscure, or otherwise unnoticed to rekindle our hope. For me, a free software drum machine produced the tiny seed that became a song. And that song became a seed that restores hope in the lives of others.

Full circle. Here's the story.

I downloaded a free piece of rhythm software. It seemed simple to use, and I thought it had the potential to be used as a part of my recordings and live productions. I wanted to modernize my sound, so I thought the sequenced drums would help.

As I explored the software, I came across some drum patterns. I don't like to use the presets, but one of the patterns caught my ear, and I went for my guitar.

I had been mucking about with a chord/rhythm pattern, and the sound from the drum application closed the loop and allowed me to move ahead with the idea.

As I looped through the pattern, the following words popped into my head.

Time and again,
You listen to me, time and again.
And I'm calling out to You.
Time and again,
You have heard our cries,
And we put our faith in You.
(Terry Posthumus, "Time and Again")

Here's the thing about those words. I wrote them a couple of weeks after Ezekiel died.

I called a good friend and sang the song over the phone. He asked me when I had written it, and I said, "Just now." Taken aback, he asked, "How is it that you're able to write a song like that at a time like this? Your son just died. You're grieving, and this is what comes out? I'm blown away by God's goodness and your willingness to let Him work through you."

Here's what I wrote when describing the song:

Throughout my life, there have been many trials and tribulations. There have been times of light and extreme darkness. There have been times when I have felt that things are good, and conversely, there have been times that it has felt like all was lost. But no matter what life has presented me, I know this to be true: anytime, anyplace, any circumstance, God hears me, and He answers my prayers.

This might seem a bit out of place in the scope of the story. But I see it as a part of the overall narrative. A vital part.

God worked through my talents and skills to encourage me. He showed me that He was present and accounted for. The Spirit inspired me to write that song when hope and inspiration were at a deficit in my life. He used my musical meanderings and gave me something of substance to share with those who are lost and hopeless. He took something incomplete and brought it full circle.

And here's what He did with it.

"Time and Again" became my first song to get traction on radio, and it played steadily for months. Millions of people heard the message of hope instilled through this song. It's even been broadcast in places where Christians are persecuted and worse. It has gone beyond my wildest imagination.

All of that from a place of grief and diminished hope.

Hope Deferred

As I stated earlier, those were the darkest of days. It was during this period of my life that I almost lost faith. During this time, I felt like I was in free fall.

But the love of God, family, friends, and a caring community caught me and held on. I felt it. I knew it. The presence of God, as evidenced through inspiration and creativity, let me know that He was near. As close as my thoughts.

So, the light didn't completely burn out.

I still had hope. And now, it meant even more to me.

You see, this hope was different. In this case, I hope that I will see Ezekiel again in eternity. Only this time, there will be no genetic defects, no brokenness, and no departures.

When I see Ezekiel again, it will be in eternity. It will be as if we have never been apart. Pain and sorrow have no place there.

I look forward to that day.

We said goodbye to Ezekiel in the NICU. But the story doesn't end there. The NICU has become the "When I See You."

Hope deferred.

In my daughter Kara's story, she needed a miracle; to have the holes in her heart healed. In Ezekiel's account, I needed the miracle; to have my broken heart healed. God was faithful in both cases, which is why I'm able to share this story of hope.

Same God. Same hope.

But wait, there's more. In my experience, the theme isn't merely a contrast of hope deferred or realized. It's more complicated than that. Every situation is different from the one before it. And that means there's no formula or "one size fits all" answer for loss and grief.

That idea was yet to be challenged as I faced a "giant" that would threaten my faith to the core.

Chapter 5
Home Is Where
the Story Begins...

June 28, 2005. A moving day like none before. This was the day we took possession of our dream house. The house on the hill. A quaint little brick house with enough bedrooms for our expansive family. There was an outbuilding on the property that was perfect for my music school. The property had lots of trees and plenty of garden space. So Lorraine could transfer her variegated perennials and fieldstone.

My family had lived in a duplex with three bedrooms up to that point. We made the most of it, but that's not much space for a family of ten. I taught my music students there, so it was bursting at the seams. We had no place to move because we were packed in like sardines.

It was time for a bigger house. We had outgrown, overflowed, and overrun the little duplex.

I'll never forget driving past the "dream house" and noticing it was up for sale. We had driven by thousands of times, but it was like I saw it for the first time on that day. I knew it was going to be ours. After taking Lorraine for a quick cruise past the house, she agreed.

I should let you know I can be impulsive. It's an apt description of me. I can act with spontaneity. I land somewhere between whimsical and capricious—definitely not mechanical or predictable.

In the case of this house, I saw the sign on the front lawn, called the real estate agent, and made an offer. The seller accepted our offer within forty-eight hours, and the moving day was set.

For the first time in my somewhat tumultuous life, I felt as though we had arrived. You must understand. This was a massive move for

Lorraine and me. We were moving from the battered duplex to one of our town's most beautiful century homes. We were relocating from one of the backstreets to the main drag. Like the Jeffersons from the 'seventies sitcom, we were "moving on up."

Moving Day(s)

Lorraine and I had gotten married eighteen years earlier. I was nineteen. She was twenty-three and pregnant. We had nothing to our names and less than no money. We were going to be "living on love."

We married in Emo, Canada, a little town on the border of Ontario and Minnesota. But this was not the place we put down roots. London, Canada, had more to offer from an opportunity point of view.

So the day after our wedding, we packed our possessions in the car and headed to south-western Ontario. When we arrived, we had about a hundred dollars in our pockets. But we both had jobs lined up for the following Monday morning. We lived our early days in the "express lane".

For the first couple of months after our wedding, Lorraine and I lived in the basement of my parents' condo unit. We had one little room and a bathroom, and we slept on a fold-out love seat. It wasn't much, but it was a roof over our heads.

It wasn't long before we all outgrew the idea. We needed to find a place of our own.

The first place of our own was a seedy apartment in London. We filled it up with hand-me-down furniture and moved in. Our son, Theo, was born three months later.

Four months after Theo was born, we moved to Port Perry, Canada. We needed to spread our wings, so I took a job on a chicken farm outside of town. Our house? A mobile home that sat unsheltered atop a rise. The commute was easy because the barns were less than a hundred-yards from the front door. But the winter winds battered, and the summer sun baked that little trailer house on the hill. It was quaint, but this guy and the farmer's life were like oil and water.

After facing the reality that I was not cut out for an agricultural career, we moved off the farm and back into town. We took a beautiful apartment on the second floor of a lawyer's office in downtown Port Perry. It was a lovely place with windows spanning the walls facing the east, south, and west. We felt like we were living in a chalet because we saw pine trees everywhere we looked. That place was constantly bathed in light.

This was a time of relative peace in our lives. I began to pursue music as a career, and Lorraine settled into the day-to-day life of raising two little boys. Shortly after we moved in, our son Justin was born. Lorraine loved how she could walk around our lakefront town with her vintage pram.

For four years, I explored several vocational options. I taught guitar, installed custom kitchen cabinets, and tried to start my own multilevel marketing business.

It was the first time that I felt "steady-ish." I started to play regular gigs and taught about twenty guitar students every week.

Three years later, my daughter Kara arrived. She stayed in our bedroom for the first months, but that wouldn't work forever. We needed to find a bigger place.

So we moved into a little rental house on a quiet street in Port Perry. The house had lots of room, including a workshop in the basement. I envisioned myself doing woodworking and fix-it projects. There was also room to create a music studio, and I began teaching guitar lessons in earnest. We built the "go-to" music school in the surrounding area within a short time.

All this extra space meant we could continue to build our family. We believed kids should grow up with siblings close in age. Theo and Justin were one and a half years apart, and we wanted the same companionship for Kara. So one year and four days after she was born, we welcomed our fourth child, Nicholas, into the fold.

After a few years on Sexton Street, I was sick of paying rent. I wanted to buy a home for my family. It always drove me crazy to know I was paying someone else's mortgage. From now on, we would pay our own. We became homeowners.

We packed our things and moved from the south to the north end of town. One day, we were renting a tiny house on a quiet street. The next, we owned our very own duplex on a cul-de-sac.

We had four children and thought that was it. Four seemed like a nice number. But then our friends Erik and Deborah came into our lives—and shortly after that, their daughter Racquel was born. She was so cute. So cute; in fact, the whole "we're done with having kids" thing was in grave danger for us.

"What's one more?" we thought.

And so Karissa arrived on the scene. Not without difficulty, as she was also a preemie. Lorraine had to be in the hospital on complete bed rest for weeks before Karissa was born—six weeks early. But her arrival proved to be pure joy for the entire family. In our minds, she was the consummate baby girl.

The home on the cul-de-sac was where we stayed until I discovered the dream house. While living there, I began my animation career and became a worship leader. I had the pleasure and privilege of working as a Disney animator during this time. I parlayed this into a full-time teaching position as a college professor. And it was at this point in the narrative, I had the opportunity to begin flexing my songwriting and production muscles.

Lorraine fell in love with gardening on Kenny Court. She sculpted the front lawn, creating intricate fieldstone patterns along the fence line and around the trees. She was always so happy to have her hands in the dirt, and landscaping became one of her favourite creative outlets.

She also took great joy in running our busy household. It's funny to think back on it because when we met in Bible college, she told me she was not planning on getting married. I had to do a lot of convincing back then. But here she was, finding her life's joy in raising children, running a bustling household, and pursuing her horticultural pursuits.

Of course, Karissa couldn't grow up alone, so Michael arrived on the scene twenty months later. Do you see a pattern here?

Remember, we were living in a three-bedroom duplex. Once again, we were approaching (or in some people's opinion had surpassed) critical mass for that house.

That home was a crucible. Grief overshadowed our lives for some time after we experienced the stillbirth of our daughter, Cherie. That grief was outshone by joy when we were blessed by the arrival of our twins, Lara and Jayme.

This moved our brood to tribe level, as we now had eight children—all living under the same roof with Lorraine and me. Imagine the clutter and chaos. Imagine the grocery bill.

We lived on the cul-de-sac for five years, but it was not a dead end. We left the same way we came, with great hope and ever-expanding dreams. In that home, we had experienced the full gamut of joy and sorrow; being in need and having plenty; chapters closing and others opening.

It was time for a change. It was time to move on to a life that would change the scope and perspective of everything.

The Dream House

What is it that makes a house a dream home?

Is it a century home, or is it new? Is it the location? Is it how the house is laid out, or is it the property? Maybe it's on the lakefront, or perhaps it's in the middle of town.

I'm not sure what it is for you, but it was a lot of different things for us.

For one thing, the home had to have room for our family. That's a tall order when you have eight kids. This home had space for our youngsters to have a playroom and a room for the older kids to hang out with their friends.

The house had a sunroom, which Lorraine loved, and a huge garage that would become the music school and rehearsal space. That, and there was still room for both of our cars. For me, it gave the house a tremendous amount of appeal.

It was the kind of house where we had the space to host friends and family. There was a vast and shaded backyard with a big deck.

The kid's school was close to the new house. Next door, to be exact. How convenient.

The high school was a block and a half away. How central.

Also, we never had space to retreat to in any of our other homes. In this house, we had an office and a sitting room.

Oh, and storage galore.

This house checked all the boxes for us, and we were so excited to make it our home.

For five years, we experienced ups and downs in that home. My daughter, Elissa, was born. Our business grew to over 140 music students. Our oldest son got married two years after we moved. And it was while we lived there that we went through our journey with Ezekiel.

But what happens when your dream home becomes the place where you face your fears? It can happen in the blink of an eye. What happens when the dream becomes a nightmare? It happened so quickly.

Zero to Sixty

I like to call home as I leave work. It's nice to get caught up. Besides, my commute is quite far and can get pretty dull.

One autumn day, I called home to touch base and give my ETA, but it wasn't Lorraine who answered the phone. One of my older kids picked up and seemed concerned.

They told me Lorraine wasn't home, and they didn't know where she was or when she would be back. They were worried, but I told them everything was okay. The older kids were home, so I knew the youngsters were cared for.

The truth is, this was out of the ordinary, and I felt uneasy. It was strange for Lorraine to go out without telling me where she was. It was troubling that she hadn't made arrangements with the kids.

What if something had happened to her? Lorraine didn't have a driver's license. We lived in a smallish town, and she couldn't have walked too far. So why was she gone so long?

It's incredible how the mind works. I went from feeling fine to fearful in the blink of an eye, like zero to sixty, lickety-split. I checked in every fifteen minutes and asked the kids to have her call me when she got home.

When I arrived home, she still wasn't back from wherever she was. My fears ramped up at that point. I drove around town looking for her. Anxiety was getting the best of me.

After a fruitless search, I headed home to find she had walked into the house a few minutes before I pulled in.

I was relieved and upset at the same time. The whole thing had been weird, and I wanted to know what was going on. Where had Lorraine been? Why hadn't she told the kids she was going out? What happened?

I wasn't in the best frame of mind. Instead of being a supportive husband, I let my heightened emotions speak first.

I wish I hadn't reacted that way. It's always better to listen more than you speak. It would have been better for me to trust God. The whole thing would've gone more smoothly.

When I was able to harness my emotions and listen, Lorraine told me she had been at the doctor's office. She hadn't thought the appointment would take so long. She said she hadn't told me about the meeting because she didn't want me to worry.

Worry about what? What could there possibly be to worry about?

She told me she had felt a lump in her breast and went to the doctor to get it checked out. And that was the beginning of the end of our time in the "dream house." And it all happened so fast.

Nothing in all the comings and goings of our life had quite the same impact on our family. I thought, *It isn't supposed to be this way.* Lorraine looked and felt well. We had recovered from the grief that came after the death of Ezekiel. Things were starting to stabilize. We had found some semblance of solidity for the first time in our lives.

It all happened so fast. The following year and a half flew by with diagnoses, prognoses, surgeries, and treatments.

First came the biopsy, which came back as HER2-positive. Both lumps were cancerous.

Lorraine and I gathered the children in the living room to break the news. It frightened the kids so much. Cancer is not a nice word. I remember them crying on the sofa as we tried to console and reassure them. They were so scared, but we decided to answer all their questions. It was such a hard thing to do. We gathered around Lorraine, held each other, and prayed.

Cancer. How could it be? Lorraine was young and healthy. She had breastfed all the kids, which should reduce the chance of breast cancer. It just didn't make sense.

She was immediately scheduled for a lumpectomy and had a lymph node removed for testing. This proved to be more difficult than anticipated.

Lorraine developed an infection in the area where the lump and lymph node had been removed. The infection became septic, and Lorraine had to undergo IV antibiotic treatments. She was very sick at that time, to the point that we worried about her life. It took a long time for her to heal, and the process was exhausting for her.

Next came the MRI and mammogram. From there, we would get a prognosis and treatment plan.

I'll never forget our first visit to the cancer centre. I was struck by the kindness and efficiency of those who worked there. But that was not what left the most profound impression on me.

As I looked around the building, it became clear that cancer doesn't discriminate. I'm not sure what I expected to see, but I was shocked by what I observed. The reality hit me like a ton of bricks. Young and old. Rich and poor. All races, creeds, and colours were represented there. It was very sobering to witness this "United Nations" representation. All united in their battle against a pandemic known as cancer.

After Lorraine had healed from the septic infection, the testing commenced, and her treatment plan was laid out. She was going to undergo a round of chemotherapy and limited radiation treatments. A total mastectomy and reconstruction would follow this.

That was hard. Watching my wife deal with the sickness that came after her treatments took its toll. The whole family walked that tough road.

Some moments stand out in my memory.

Three Things

They say bad things happen in threes. This notion is deeply embedded in our psyche, and anecdotal evidence supports it. I'm not saying it's true, but I'm going to share this part of the story by telling you about three significant losses during this time of our life. These losses impacted our lives with considerable force and threatened to undo us. But God was faithful in each case, and He either walked with or carried us through.

If you had the pleasure of meeting Lorraine in this life, you know one of her outstanding features was her luxurious hair. She was known for it, and it left a strong impression on everyone. Her hair was like her crown. She was proud of it without being vain about it, and for her to lose her hair was an earth-shattering thing for her.

The pain was lessened when we were able to find her a wig. We were both very nervous about this part of the process. The cost was prohibitive, and Lorraine wasn't sure about wearing a wig that didn't look like her own hair. But when we went to the store, I found a wig on the clearance rack that looked like Lorraine's hair. It had been there for a long time because it was very dusty. The woman who owned the store had forgotten it was even there. After a cleaning and cut, the wig looked precisely like Lorraine's hair. What a blessing.

A little bit of grace in the middle of trying times. It's like how we know that the sun is shining behind the clouds, and then we see the rays shine through. The whole process fostered hope to see us through the next steps.

Although the divinely perfect discovery of Lorraine's wig made us feel very loved, it didn't reduce the shock when her hair started falling out. That was a sad day at our house. Lorraine had cut her hair to begin wearing the wig, but it caught us off guard when her hair started falling out very quickly. When she asked me to shave her head, we sat in the living room of our dream home and wept together as I cut it all off for her.

The living room had been the centre of family activity. It was where we opened Christmas gifts, hosted guests, and watched movies with the kids. And there we sat, cutting off Lorraine's hair. The house lost some of its lustre that day. The dream home facade was collapsing and had taken on a "real world" vibe with all its brokenness. This is difficult for those who are romantically inclined. When you remove the rose-coloured glasses, reality can be harsh and glaring.

Another part of the journey that stands out to me is the whole reconstructive process after Lorraine had a total mastectomy. Lorraine faced the surgery with bravery and grace, but it was very difficult for her. We had many discussions about how she had fed the children with her breasts. She felt like she would lose a big part of her womanhood due to the removal. And although there would be a reconstruction, she was worried about feeling "fake."

She had already gone through the process of losing her hair. Now she was about to lose her breasts, as well. And for every loss, a fake solution. Wigs and implants. It wasn't the same to her, and she felt the loss and grief of it.

The day of the surgery was a long one. We arrived at the hospital first thing in the morning and waited what seemed an interminable length of time for Lorraine to be called in. We tried to show a brave face in that place, but it was hard to keep fear at bay. Lorraine had the mastectomy and reconstructive surgery on the same day. We understood it could be done but had a difficult time imagining it. She went through the entire process in twenty-f0ur hours.

As I sit here today, it's difficult for me to remember all the details. I wasn't thinking about recording every event and associated emotion. But I can remember Lorraine was affected deeply. What a grievous loss for a woman. Let me be very clear when I tell you that reconstruction does not equal recovery. I'm not sure she ever fully recovered. Physical healing is one thing. Healing of the soul and spirit is quite another. I would say in hindsight that a part of Lorraine's heart broke that day. And I don't think it ever fully healed.

Our bedroom became the recovery room, and with that in mind, I wish we had never bought the house. The room was upstairs and apart from the rest of the house. It was nice if you were looking for quiet but isolating if you were lonely. Life happened downstairs, and it felt like a million miles away when you were stuck up there. In that sense, the "dream house" became an isolation ward for Lorraine.

This leads me to the third loss.

There came a day when we got an "all-clear" message from her oncologist. We rejoiced with friends and family as we thought the worst was behind us.

But cancer is costly. The costs hit the soul, spirit, body, and pocketbook hard. The journey is exhausting. The wear and tear on your heart and soul are palpable. And although we live in a country that covers healthcare, there are ancillary costs that can crush a family.

This was the case in our situation. We amassed quite a bit of debt throughout the year and a half that Lorraine was treated. We got so behind that we were in financial jeopardy, and it became clear that the payment on the dream house was becoming an anchor that was going to sink us. Our money was running out long before the month did. Something had to be done, and quickly.

We decided to sell the home. I called the bank and told them of our intentions. I asked that our mortgage payments be held back for ninety days while we took the time to stage and sell the house. An agreement was struck, and the clock started counting down.

Many people came through the house, but their interest only seemed to be skin deep. How is it that the home we enjoyed so much couldn't pique the interest of those who walked through? I was starting to worry that we would run out of time. If that happened, we would have to turn the keys over to the bank. The very idea of it made me feel ill.

I prayed about what to do, and I was sure we were doing the right thing. It wasn't that God specifically told me to sell the house. It seemed like it was the right thing to do. I had been so sure of it. Now that we were coming to the deadline, the pressure was on. There were some sleepless nights during those weeks.

Then, out of nowhere, some friends approached us about buying the house. We had no idea they were interested. They made an offer, we accepted, and a moving date was set.

Six years after buying our dream home, we had to sell it. That sounds like a sad story. But as I look back on it from this perspective, I can see grace was at work. And although it seemed like a desperate contingency at the time, I'm able to take hope from it today. It would be easy to see this as a failure. I have struggled with that idea many times. But we were unshackled in many ways when we moved out of that house.

Remember how I said the house had lost its lustre? The financial burden had become a point of contention, and it was too great to bear. We were starting every month so far behind there was no way we would be able to pull out of the tailspin.

We also had no idea what was coming down the road because Lorraine would be hit with an even more significant health challenge in the next year. This time, she would not be isolated from the family. The home we moved into put her right in the action where the household was concerned. Again, I never thought about that until well after the fact. But what a blessing that was. Our master bedroom was right off the kitchen in a ranch-style bungalow. The family was within earshot and arm's length.

It sucked to lose the dream house. It was hard to say goodbye to something we had worked hard for. I could wax about how a home is where the heart is or something like that. It's true, but the idea of it held little consolation. It was one of those "everything comes into question" moments. We made the best of it, but it hurt to hand those keys over at the end of the day.

You may be wondering where the hope is in this story. I understand. Writing this chapter was difficult.

But a wise friend told me that there doesn't have to be an epiphany or lesson in the narrative. Sometimes, the simple fact that you survived shouts from the mountaintop. There's no way for me to make this story soft and pretty. It's rather blunt. I thought we had found our dream home, but it turned out to be a rather painful chapter in my life in the final analysis.

By God's grace, I am still standing. I still believe He meets our needs and even gives us the desire of our hearts. I haven't given up on the fact that He is faithful and "in all things God works for the good of those who love him" (Romans 8:28). I haven't and will not surrender myself to fate or the whims of the universe. I cling to the belief that "my God will meet all your needs according to the riches of his glory in Christ Jesus" (Philippians 4:19).

No Matter What

As the parent of many children, I have listened to countless kids' songs. They are beautiful in their simplicity and repetitiveness. The messages are simple, but that doesn't water down the truth they tell.

In one song, the message is it's a good morning, and it's going to be a good day. Why? Because God is good.

Simple. Straight to the point. So, let's look at this story from that perspective.

We found and bought our "dream home"—God is good.

We enjoyed five years of peace and progress—God is good.

Lorraine was diagnosed with breast cancer—even then, God is good.

We almost lost her when the surgical incision went septic—God is good.

She went through a year of treatments harsher than the disease—still, God is good.

We got the "all-clear"—yes! God is good.

Lorraine had a total mastectomy and reconstructive surgery—God is good.

We had financial challenges—God is good.

We had to sell our dream home—God is good.

We were able to sell the home and pay off any debt associated with the house—God is good.

When all seems well, and life takes another abrupt turn, God is good even then!

"For the LORD is good and his love endures forever; his faithfulness continues through all generations" (Psalm 100:5).

Chapter 6
You Alone Are My Salvation

Happily, she doesn't have cancer anymore,
so everything is going back to normal.
(Karissa Posthumus, 2011)

What Lies Beneath the Surface

After selling the dream house, we moved into a quaint little bungalow. Renters once again.

With that, we went about the business of resetting and restarting. The previous years had been tumultuous, and we needed some time to catch our breath. Although it was a step or two backwards financially, we were thankful to have a roof over our heads.

The house was small but oozed with potential. We were down to three bedrooms for our large family. Being a bit of an optimist, I looked at it this way: what it lacked in space, the home made up for in a finished basement and a fireplace.

Days after moving in at the new address, I helped my kids, Nicholas and Kara, move to Toronto, Canada. Kara had decided to go to Bible college, and Nick headed for a career in film production.

Those were some hectic days.

They were also sad days for Nick and Kara. They moved out of their family home (our dream home) and never had a "home of their own" to return to. That was a rude awakening for them and a challenging period in their lives. There are many types of loss and grief. For Nick and Kara, it was the loss of their childhood home. They would now be guests whenever they came "home" for a visit.

Life carried on for the rest of the family. School started for the kids, my music school opened again, and I began another semester at the college. Lorraine got busy getting us settled into the new place. We had made the best of a challenging situation. The tiny house on Bay Street was beginning to feel like home.

As for cancer, we believed that it was behind us. We had gotten the all-clear and hoped never to hear that word again. Lorraine had come through the reconstructive surgery process with flying colours. Her crown of hair had grown back to its epic proportions. We were feeling confident about her health.

After a busy fall and Christmas season, 2012 arrived. We had settled in, and with that, we were enjoying life and getting back to some semblance of normal. Winter and spring passed in peace.

With the arrival of summer, Lorraine tended her new garden. She knew this would make the place feel like home for us. She began doing that fieldstone thing she did.

But there was an insidious disease working beneath the surface. It sort of crept up on us.

When she started to experience lower back pain, we chalked it up to the yard work. Nothing an ibuprofen pill wouldn't fix. But when the pain started to become chronic, we looked into massage therapy. Lorraine began to take lots of painkillers, and I was very concerned.

That September, my daughter, Kara, decided to stay home for the year. She felt she needed to be around to help her mother, so she took the year off school. She helped with the kids and assisted Lorraine with the duties around the house. Little did we know how important this personal sacrifice would become.

Our Thanksgiving 2012 family photo was the last one ever taken. Lorraine had arranged for a photographer to come by the house, and she staged us for the "perfect family photo." Theo and his wife, Laura, were leaving for Australia. Lorraine wanted to capture the moment for posterity. I suspect she knew something was wrong. That Thanksgiving was the last holiday we celebrated together as an entire family.

Throughout October, the pain worsened, and there were days Lorraine couldn't get out of bed. I was getting anxious. I wondered whether she had pinched a nerve or she might have a degenerative disk in her back. We had no idea what was lurking in the shadows.

The Monster Reveals Itself

We enjoy movie nights, and the kids and I were watching a movie together when I heard a blood-curdling scream from the other side of the house. Terrified, I ran to the bathroom, where I found Lorraine collapsed in a heap on the floor and shrieking in pain. I tried to help her, but any attempt to assist her only increased the pain. I told Kara to take the kids downstairs to the relative isolation of the family room and called 911.

Even the expert hands of the paramedics caused Lorraine to cry out in pain. This was not good. Despite her screams of pain, they managed to move her into the ambulance. I followed, all the while wondering, *What's going on?*

We spent the night in the E.R. as the doctor tried to treat Lorraine for back spasms. Several painkilling and muscle-relaxing drugs were used but to no effect. Out of desperation, I asked the doctor to check for kidney stones. The doctor agreed and ordered the test. The test revealed Lorraine's kidneys were functioning at thirty percent. She was in danger of kidney failure.

The doctors transferred her to the regional hospital. There she underwent more testing and treatments. She responded well, and her renal function returned. But her kidneys were not the only problem.

With her kidney function restored, the doctors tested Lorraine for cardiopulmonary issues. They worried she might have had a heart attack or pulmonary embolism. But there was no connection between the symptoms and her cardio health.

When the oncologists approached us, I couldn't imagine why. I had no clue about what metastatic cancer was—yet. Besides, Lorraine had gotten an all-clear from her previous stint with cancer. Over the next few days, she would undergo a CT scan, MRI, and bone density scan.

I met with the oncologist a couple of days later. When he showed me Lorraine's bone scan, I was shocked. Stage four metastatic breast cancer. It was everywhere. Her entire spine, ribs, and pelvis showed black marks. It was even in her skull. We now understood why Lorraine had experienced so much pain in her back.

All this took place in one week. We had been through a lot in our twenty-five years of marriage, but nothing like this.

Lorraine did not want to go through the harsh chemotherapy treatments again. She wanted to come home and feel well enough to enjoy her family and friends. I struggled with this. I wanted to fight the cancer. Lorraine seemed resigned to the fact it had returned with such ferocity. Early on, she was at peace with whatever the outcome might be. This did not sit well with me, and I began researching options and alternatives. I was determined to do whatever I could to help my bride overcome this illness.

For starters, we decided we wouldn't focus on the prognosis or the outcome. We weren't going to give in to fear. Instead, we purposed to focus on gratitude. Every day is a gift. We knew that from our experiences with Cherie and Ezekiel.

The Fight of Our Lives ... But Not Alone
Sixteen days after Lorraine had the fall, she came home. We used the time to plan and conspire against the disease. We researched and consulted about alternative cancer treatments, narrowed in on a few approaches, and developed a regimen to follow.

Our treatment plan was a simple protocol, and the goal was to cure her cancer. We consulted with an M.D. who specialized in naturopathic/alternative cancer treatments. We were also in regular contact with a naturopath and dietary expert. We were getting regular clinical feedback on our protocol. Aiming for a cure was audacious, but it was our target. We operated under the belief that it was God who knows the number of our days. That undergirding truth became our manifesto and creed.

We purchased a high-quality therapeutic gel memory foam bed. Lorraine was happy and comfortable, enjoying her home and family.

At first, she was using prescription painkillers. Within a short time, she no longer required drugs. The protocol paid dividends immediately. She was without pain. Not only that, she enjoyed the juicing aspect of her regimen. She always loved making smoothies for the kids, and now I was making fresh-pressed juices for her.

It's important to mention that we were not alone in the fight. Our faith community surrounded and supported us: faith, hope, and love in action. I'll never forget that, and I remain grateful to this day.

The day after Lorraine came home from the hospital, I received a call from one of the pastors in our town. He asked to drop by for a minute. When he arrived, he placed an envelope of cheques and bills in my hand. Money came from people I knew or who knew of me from the film and animation business. Our church provided meals, and our freezer had a constant flow of food going into it. Old friends would drop by, looking for ways to help. Like those who bought us a freezer to help hold the food coming in every day. Our family was well cared for. My "sugar bowl" never ran empty during those days.

"The most wonderful time of the year" approached quickly, and Christmas planning had begun all around us. But we were behind. My attention was elsewhere. There were many adjustments and new routines associated with Lorraine's care. But, like my experiences as a fatherless child, others stepped up and stood in the gap for us.

One Friday evening, while going about the business of caring for the family, I heard a lot of noise on the roof. Who was up there? Was it Santa? Excited, the kids and I headed to the front entrance to check on what was going on. As we approached, the doorbell rang. Opening the door, I gasped. With a hearty "Excuse me", a couple of families from our church walked in with a giant Christmas tree. Next came the train of people bearing gifts and groceries. It seemed to go on and on. The noise on the roof was not the clamour of reindeer feet. Two fellows from our church were up there, installing Christmas lights.

My work community also showed us what generous love looked like. The vice president of human resources called me into her office in early December. I had missed quite a bit of work and had some concerns about the nature of the meeting. The meeting turned out to be an incredible demonstration of support and generosity. First, she told me I had the time needed to take care of my family. And I didn't need to worry about interruptions to my salary and benefits. Finally, she asked me to submit a Christmas Wish List. A couple of days before Christmas, I filled the van to the roof with gifts from my colleagues.

There's more. So much more. But to give you a clear idea of the generosity, it took us several hours to open all the gifts we had received. The kindness was overwhelming.

Friends and family showed themselves to be stalwart and faithful. They stood with us through good times and bad times. Timely words of encouragement edified us. Gifts of food and money poured into our home. We were able to provide the best care for Lorraine as monetary donations flowed in from around the world.

Without fail, my friend Dan took me out for wings every Thursday night. We would talk about whatever I wanted or needed to talk about; what a gift his friendship was to me. Lorraine's oldest and best friend, Elaine, came to spend a week with her. She spent most of the time sitting on the bed with Lorraine. They laughed and cried, reminisced, and dreamed. They encouraged each other with the love of friendship.

Our sisters created a rotating schedule to stay with us and help with the running of our household. What a gift they were to us. When push came to shove, these beautiful women of God showed up to help their loved ones.

The gestures of love were perpetual and prolific in those days. I had never felt so loved and cared for.

All the support we received allowed me to focus on Lorraine's care. As her primary caregiver, I managed her treatment protocol. I took responsibility for bathing and assisting her with her care. I took her to appointments and ran all the errands.

While the flow of love and support was unreal, these were still challenging days. Being confined to her bed frustrated Lorraine. The hours dragged out for her. Tumours inundated her bones, so she had to be there. If she moved too much or even the wrong way, she could break a bone: worst-case scenario, a compression fracture in one of her vertebrae.

These are not the things you dream of when you're young and falling in love. You never imagine the "for better or worse" or "in sickness and in health" aspect of your marriage vows—until you face it. Then you have a decision to make.

With God's help, I did everything I could to fulfill my vows to Lorraine. I supported my wife's spirit, soul, and body in these trying times. We would see this through, come what may. We were in this together all the way.

All the gestures of love and kindness created an air of peace and contentment, even in this storm. That and the protocol seemed to be producing favourable results on several fronts. Lorraine had no pain. She had good energy, although this created restlessness for her. The constant flow of traffic through our home seemed to lift her spirits. As the kids opened their Christmas gifts, she joined the family on the couch. She seemed to be gaining some strength and mobility and could occasionally move around the house.

But when things are going well, we tend to let our guard down. It takes something forceful or even catastrophic to stop or divert strong momentum.

We were beginning to think we were out of the woods and that it was a matter of time for her body to win this pitched battle with cancer.

We had no idea what was coming. The light at the end of the tunnel turned out to be a train.

To Have and To Hold, From This Day Forward, for Better or Worse, Richer or Poorer, in Sickness and Health

After New Year's, we received some encouraging news from Lorraine's follow-up bone scan. The cancer had not progressed. Considering the prognosis a few months earlier, we had cause for celebration. It felt like we were on the right track. As I said, we thought we were winning this fight.

With all the help our sisters provided, I felt I could go back to work. Time might have stood still for us, but the students' year was on the line. I was the program coordinator for the animation diploma. The teachers and students needed me to be present. My absence was taking a toll at the college.

I decided to go back to work with Lorraine's sister staying at the house. She had settled into the routines, and the household functioned efficiently. The children were comfortable with her, and we knew they were in a good place with family around.

I would still be available to take care of Lorraine's appointments and errands. But I was able to return to work at the beginning of the new semester.

It felt like we were winning. Support in food, finances, time, and resources continued to pour in. It made our days brighter and better.

Lorraine was still spending most of her waking hours in bed. The tumours were still present, which made her bones very fragile. Yet she remained pain-free, which was a tremendous blessing unto itself. Stage four cancer patients often take high doses of Percocet. Not Lorraine. Eleven weeks into her treatment protocol, this continued to be the case.

As time wore on, Lorraine grew restless. She wanted to be mobile, and being confined to the bed was frustrating. She wanted to move around the house a bit. So I would support her, and together, we would walk to the living room to sit by the fire and visit with the children.

She enjoyed a slow dance. Occasionally, I would play "The Lady in Red" by Chris DeBurgh. She loved that song, and we talked, laughed, and "danced." It gave me so much hope to see her smiling and moving. I felt like we might be winning.

We did everything possible to ensure that Lorraine didn't feel cooped up in the bedroom. She loved flowers, so we made sure the room was well appropriated in the floral sense. Lorraine began to develop restless legs syndrome (RLS). She wanted to get up and move about. Most of all, she wanted a bath … a nice, relaxing, hot bath. I purchased some gel pads for her to sit on in the bathtub and some fizzy bath bombs. It was helpful, for sure, but the shaking legs were beginning to wear us thin.

Early on, the hospital offered us a bed to be brought into our home, but we decided our bedroom (our bed) would be the place Lorraine would stay. We weren't the kind of couple who liked to be apart.

We shared our bedroom throughout this entire journey. It was what we wanted— to be together. And although we were not able to be intimate in the same way we had in days past, we hugged and held each other every night. It also proved convenient, as I was close by when she needed help at night.

But the RLS was becoming problematic, and it began to take a toll on both of us. Neither of us was getting the right kind or amount of sleep.

A lack of sleep is terrible on many levels. I'm not talking about staying up late one night and "paying for it" the next day. Lack of sleep, in this case, was night after night, week after week. It began to wear us down, and despair crept in. Our lack of sleep wore at our defences.

I knew Lorraine needed her sleep. If she was going to recover, she needed to have all systems functioning optimally. We needed to stay positive and patient. But positivity and patience are some of the first things to go when there is a chronic lack of sleep.

I remember one night in particular. We hadn't slept well for a few weeks, and Lorraine's legs were particularly shaky that night. To top it off, she had to rouse me several times to help her to relieve herself. At one point, I had fallen into a decent sleep when Lorraine woke me to help her again. I did not react well.

Throughout the process of helping Lorraine, I was abrupt and upset. I remember going outside to deal with the matter. Looking at the heavens, I muttered things I will not repeat. I was angry with God, and I was spinning out of control. A lack of sleep will cause a person to make terrible judgment calls.

When I got back to the room, Lorraine looked at me and said, "I need you to smile at me. No matter what. I need to know that you love me." I smiled all right—a sarcastic and empty smile. Then I crawled back into bed, said a cursory "I love you," and tried to sleep. All the while, I was seething under the surface. Angry at God. Upset about the situation. I was not in a good place.

The following day, I got up and took a bath. While I was sitting there, Lorraine's words from the night before echoed in my mind. "I need you to smile at me." I felt like such a heel. I felt like I didn't deserve Lorraine. I knew I had hurt her and needed to make things right.

I jumped out of the bath and ran to her. I collapsed into her arms and wept. Through my tears, I apologized, over and over. I told her I was sorry. I said to her I didn't deserve her. I told her I would always be there for her, and I would still have smiles for her, no matter what.

I'm so thankful she forgave me. That was not a highlight moment for this guy. But our choices helped us get a foothold in hope. I chose to apologize and ask for forgiveness. Lorraine chose forgiveness. Together, we chose hope.

Out of Left Field ... Until Death Do Us Part

As mid-March approached, Lorraine's health took a sudden shift. She developed a nasty cough and couldn't seem to clear her lungs. Antibiotics seemed to help for a few days, but the cough returned. This time, it was worse. The cough was more persistent, and it was harder to get any relief from it.

It was concerning, but we had no idea what would happen.

I spoke to a friend about Lorraine's cough, and he cautioned me about the potential for pneumonia. He told me about the time he had broken his back and had to remain immobilized in bed for months. During that time, he had developed severe pneumonia several times. He had gotten so sick with it that his life had been in jeopardy.

With Lorraine being immobile, he warned me she could be at risk of pneumonia. Little did we know, it was a harbinger of things to come. That very night, the situation would turn a corner.

We ended the day like any other. Lorraine got up to move around a bit. I ran a bath for her, and when she finished bathing, we danced to our favourite song. After that, I tucked her back into bed, and with a kiss and a hug, we said goodnight.

I awoke in the night when I felt the bed had become wet. That was very unusual. Lorraine hadn't had a single "accident" throughout the entire sickness. I was very concerned and tried to rouse her.

No response. I checked to make sure she was breathing. I could hear that she was. But I couldn't wake her.

I changed the bedding and lay beside her. This was the last night we spent beside each other.

Morning arrived, and with it, no change in Lorraine's condition. She was not responsive. I called our family doctor, who came to the house to check on Lorraine. He told me it was the beginning of the end. He asked me to keep in close communication with him.

I couldn't understand that. How could we be dancing less than twelve hours earlier, and now, Lorraine was at death's door? It didn't add up.

The only response I got from her that day was when I told her I called Theo home from Australia. She didn't open her eyes but scowled at me. From the outset, Lorraine had determined Theo would be able to stay in Australia. She took great joy watching him enjoy the adventure of a lifetime. She did not expect death would come.

We moved Lorraine from the bedroom to the living room for her final days. The kids and I and friends and family surrounded her around the clock. She was at peace in her home. As a group of people who loved Lorraine, I remember how we gathered around her to close out the days. We would sing her favourite hymns and worship songs, cry out to God, and comfort each other. It was poignant, because we sensed the end was near, and soothing as God moved in our midst. He calmed and reassured us with perfect hope.

As Lorraine's final day began to close, we once again gathered around her to sing and pray. Her breathing had become very difficult.

While we were standing around her bed, she opened her eyes and sat up. Everyone saw it and began shouting her name. "Lorraine! Lorraine!"

But I saw what was in her eyes. She didn't have the look of someone who was arriving but of someone who was leaving.

I took her in my arms and held her tight. I said, "I love you so much, Lorraine. It's going to be okay."

With that, she breathed her last.

Pushback

I don't remember much about the days that followed. It's a blur, and I survived it, but that's about it.

The funeral director took Lorraine's body away. Soon after, I began throwing all the hospital paraphernalia on the porch and front lawn. I wanted it out of the house. With the purge complete, I sat around with my children as we wept at the pain and laughed at the good memories— tears of sadness and laughter. Everything else aside, that evening with the children was one of the best times in my life.

The next day was Elissa's birthday. So, we had a birthday party. We were all in shock, but Elissa was turning five years old. She needed a cake, a dress, some gifts, and a rousing version of "Happy Birthday."

A few days later, we celebrated Lorraine's life. There was a visitation I somehow managed to bumble through. I was in a trance-like state, but I remember a couple of things. First, there was a nasty winter storm. Yet people came from all over, driving hundreds of miles through the storm to hug and hold me up. I'll never forget that. It's a blessing to have such friends. Second, there were so many people there. We stood in that line for hours. It was exhausting, but I felt such love and support once again.

Lorraine was deeply loved, and she loved deeply. She was a loving mother who tried, in all things, to show her children the love of God. She believed in God. Her faith wasn't mere words or an act. Lorraine was the kind of friend who encouraged you in a godly way. She was always spurring those she loved to speak words of life. She carried herself with grace and dignity, and although she could be very bold, she was a humble servant of God. Lorraine was wholly dedicated to our marriage and helped me move closer to God. She left a strong and lasting impression on everyone she came in contact with.

It's little wonder that the church was so full on the day of her funeral. There wasn't a seat left in the house, and the service played on a screen in the basement overflow.

I gathered my family in the nursery beforehand. We prayed together, took a deep breath, and headed into the hushed room. I walked to the coffin, said my final farewell to Lorraine, and closed the lid.

I was able to say, "Goodbye, my love," because we had made some good choices along the way. We battled cancer for three years and kept short accounts with each other. Even in the evening when she passed away, I told the kids about how their mother and I had no "unfinished business." I'm glad that we chose to treat each other this way. The potential for anger, bitterness, resentment, and despair loomed large. I'm sure that the enemy of our souls would have loved nothing better than to throw that junk into the mix.

But we chose transparency, forgiveness, grace, and love manifested through sacrifice. There is no greater love. There was grief, but there was also strong hope.

You could have heard a pin drop in the place when the children and I walked onstage and picked up our instruments. The children and I led worship at Lorraine's funeral.

I thanked everyone for coming. I said, "This is our pushback."

And together, as a family surrounded by a community of friends and family, we sang my song:

For I know the Lord will be a shield around me,
My glory and the one who lifts my head.
And I know that You alone are my salvation.
I know that I am blessed.

When David wrote Psalm 3, he was running for his life. His son, Absalom, had become his foe and was hunting his father down.

When the situation seemed to be at its most dire, David wrote a song. I can relate. I've been there. Sometimes the only thing I can do is write a song.

What strikes me in this psalm is the theme. He wasn't whining or asking God to rescue him. It's very clear from the poetry that David believed God would restore him to his throne. He could lay his head to rest, assured he would rise in the morning. David believed God would protect him because he was the anointed king. It seemed everyone was against him. Despite this, David believed God had not abandoned him; he regarded Him as his shield—his real source of protection.

I wrote a song based on Psalm 3. It's called "You Alone Are My Salvation." I've performed this song all over the world. It's one of my most requested tunes. Many have covered and translated it into other languages. In a worship service, one of the most unique ways I've heard it played was with steel drums. I'm glad this song that has encouraged me so much has been an encouragement for so many others.

For me, the most poignant performance of this song was at Lorraine's funeral. I sang it with my children and the hundreds who had gathered to celebrate her life and bid "fare thee well." I sang to push back against cancer. There was no way death would have the final say in Lorraine's story.

I sang, trusting the Lord would shield me. I sang, hoping in the One who alone was my salvation. I sang, believing He would deliver and restore me.

He would. But there was still a rough road ahead: one that threatened to destroy me—spirit, soul, and body. And the only way that I would be saved from being wiped out was surprising to me.

Chapter 7
Wade in the Water

Wade in the water
Wade in the water, children
Wade in the water
God's gonna trouble the water.
(Negro Spiritual)

There's a story about a storm in the Gospel of Mark (Mark 4:35–41). In this story, Jesus had said to His followers, "Let's go to the other side of the lake."

Like good followers, they obeyed.

As they headed across the lake, a crazy storm whipped up into a frenzy. The Gospel account says waves were going over the boat, and water had filled the hull. Not good.

I read something like that, and I get a picture of George Clooney, his boat, and the giant wave in *The Perfect Storm*. That didn't end well.

Moving along, the story says how Jesus's followers found Him sound asleep. His head was resting on a pillow in the back of the boat. These were men of the sea. They understood the peril they were in, and they didn't understand how Jesus was sleeping. Not under these circumstances.

They asked, "Teacher, don't you care that we're drowning?"

So, Jesus stands up and speaks to the wind and the waves. He says, "Quiet. Be still."

And the wind stopped. And the waves became still.

Tropical Storm

I was in the Philippines on a short-term mission trip when I experienced my first tropical storm.

The suddenness and ferocity of it made an impression on me. One minute, I was enjoying a humid, sunny day, and the next—torrential rain.

At the time, I was sitting on a covered porch, feasting on seafood, coconut, and adobo dishes. Out of nowhere, there was a cool breeze followed by a blanket of rain. I had never experienced anything like it. We had to yell at the top of our lungs to continue conversations. It was startling and unusual. The rain pounded the roof, sounding like the roar of Niagara Falls, and then, as quickly as it had started, it was over.

We stayed relatively close to the ocean—close enough to hear the waves. And as soon as the rain stopped, the waves and humidity ratcheted up a notch or two. The beach called to me. It would be such sweet relief to be able to jump into the water on such a sultry day.

We headed towards the beach, and as we got closer, the sound of the surf grew louder. I could hear the waves crashing onto the shore. The closer I got; the more excitement stirred up in me. The storm had whipped the surf into a frenzy, and I could hear that the waves were huge. What the guys and I saw when we got to the beach led to a unanimous decision.

Body Surfing

I'm six feet four inches tall. The waves were higher than that.

The cooling water and fun it promised couldn't happen soon enough. We ran into the water with reckless abandon and started playing in the waves. I felt like a kid again. What a blast!

My version of bodysurfing looked like this. I waited for a wave to propel me forward and then swam with all my might. It was awe-inspiring to feel that power and freedom. I'd never seen or experienced anything like it. The relentless waves pushed to shore at an alarming rate, and once I "caught a wave," I was powerless. I was along for the ride.

What I called bodysurfing that day probably looked hilarious to any-one who knew better. I'm not exactly lithe or graceful. I'm sure I may have appeared to be a pale beached whale thrashing about in the waves.

As carefree as it felt, there was a dangerous side to our water games. They say, "It's all fun and games until…." I was about to experience one of the most frightening things in my life.

The idea was that everyone would see who could ride a wave the farthest. The fun soon turned into a full-on competition. And as the next wave approached—which was a doozy, by the way—I did my best to catch it.

Things did not go well. The looming wave pounded me down towards the ocean floor. It took me by surprise. I managed to get my elbows up and prevented my head from hitting the sand. But it was utterly disorienting, and panic set it. There was sand swirling around, and I couldn't see the surface. My body was being tossed around like a rag doll. I hadn't taken a breath to prepare. My feet couldn't find the ocean floor for the briefest of moments, and I thought, *This could be the end.* It was terrifying.

After what seemed an eternity, I broke through the surface. I checked to make sure I could move everything and breathed a sigh of relief. The adrenaline was pumping. I was glad I had survived, but the whole thing left me shaken. There would be no more bodysurfing for this guy.

In most situations, that would have been it for me. Danger is not my middle name.

But on that day, I took a different approach. I'm not sure what my motivation was. I've mulled it over many times because it is outside my character to take physical risks.

After one of my kids falls down the stairs, I'm the kind of guy who bans stair usage for the foreseeable future.

I joke.

After having the scare of my life, I decided to change the game. With caution, I began wading into the water to see if I could withstand the power of the waves. I tried walking into them side-on. I tried going backwards. I even tried tucking my chin into my chest and walking straight into the wave.

If I wasn't in too deep and braced myself, I could stand against the power of the waves. But if I waded in past my waist, I was likely to get pounded. I learned I could lean into the waves and survive the onslaught. But if I stood ramrod straight, I got knocked over.

It was a sobering experience to get knocked into the surf. It was a learning experience, too—one that I would draw on six years later—to lean into the waves.

Waves of Grief

Grief hit me like the wave that drove me into the seabed. And it left me gasping for air.

After Lorraine passed away, I experienced sudden and ferocious bouts of grief. The pain of the grief was palpable. What I was feeling seemed like a heart attack. It was debilitating. It scared the crap out of me, to be blunt. I came close to calling 911 because I thought this was the end of me.

I was completely disoriented.

I had panic attacks regularly.

As I said, I thought I was dying.

When grief hit me, there were times it knocked me to the ground. Often, I felt like I couldn't breathe. I sobbed and gasped for air. There were times it felt like an elephant was sitting on my chest. At other times, it felt like someone had cut my chest open with a dull and rusty blade.

Grief incapacitated me as quickly as the storm hit when I was in the Philippines. There was no warning for this unrestrained sorrow. It terrified me because I had young children at home. They needed me, and it felt like I was not going to be able to be there for them.

At times I hid in my bedroom. I didn't want my little kids to see me curled up and bawling my eyes out. I shut myself away because I didn't want to frighten the children with my pain.

I had to do something. The kids needed me, but I was useless to them.

Everyone who had been there in the days following Lorraine's death had gone back to their lives. I got it. Life goes on, and it continued for me, too. I was now on my own, trying to show a "brave face." But inside, I was freaking out. I was a dad with five children ranging from five to thirteen. Each of them was grieving. All were trying to figure out what living looked like now that their mom was gone.

They needed me—and I was stuck in grief and panic. It wasn't good. Something needed to happen, and fast.

So I prayed.

And while I was praying, the memory of the waves in the Philippines came to mind. This baffled me. It was weird. Have you ever wondered why something, in particular, comes to mind? I was crying out to God in desperation, and my mind chose to wander to a time that I got knocked around by waves.

But no.

It wasn't about the storm's powerful impact or the aftermath of the waves. It was what happened next.

The part where I began wading into the water.

God was reminding me about facing the waves.

Being aware of where I stood concerning them.

Leaning into the wave. Pushing back against the fear and the force of it.

That's what I needed to do about the grief. I needed to face the fear and push back against the panic.

The grief could hit me at any time and in any place. I had no control over it. I could be eating at a restaurant or driving down the road, sitting at the dinner table or talking on the phone.

It was ruthless and unpredictable.

It was like the wave that almost ended me when I was bodysurfing. Relentless. Unyielding.

But I remembered I didn't get beat up by the waves when I waded into the water. I didn't feel afraid when I pushed back against the force of the wave.

Through my prayer, God showed me how to deal with grief.

I had to face it head-on, trusting He would lead me through it.

I began to press in through prayer because I saw the first glimmers of hope. I knew God was in this. He was "in the water" with me. I felt sure He would hear and answer my prayer.

Through prayer, I concluded I needed to go to Grand Rapids, Michigan, where Lorraine and I had met. We were both students at Reformed Bible College (RBC). I met her in September, and I had purchased her a promise ring by Christmas.

Less than a year later, we married.

Grand Rapids was Terry and Lorraine's geographical, spiritual, and relational birthplace. I knew I had to go there.

I had to walk where we had walked. I had to pray where we had talked.

I was so sure God was leading me in this that I prayed a bold prayer. I asked God to heal me while I was in Grand Rapids.

Let me be very clear. I prayed a particular prayer; I desired that God would heal my heart and soul to the point that there would be no scars. I wasn't seeking a temporary fix. I wasn't trying to steep myself in nostalgia for memory's sake. I wasn't sure how He would do it. But I knew that I needed the kind of restoration only God can accomplish.

Sometimes in grief, it's easy to dwell in memories. This isn't what I wanted. I wasn't trying to drum up some cathartic experience. I hoped and believed that God would answer this prayer:

To fill the holes. To repair the rending my heart had gone through. To renew my strength. To make my heart as good as new.

I chose to "wade into the waters" of grief with its foreboding surf. I packed my bag and headed to where it all began.

I was hopeful because I was sure of the One leading me.

Ghost on the Water

Ignoring the counsel of good friends is dicey. It's a risky proposition to ignore signs of danger. We can learn good things from the combined experiences of others, and it's a dangerous thing to ignore precedent.

When I left for Grand Rapids, I had a couple of friends concerned about what I was doing. One thought I was throwing myself into peril. Another told me he thought I was going to have a nervous breakdown. Yet another said it was way too soon, and it would likely break me beyond repair.

Another person told me there was no way God could heal my heart in that time frame. They thought I was presumptuous toward God and had twisted Scripture for my purposes. I was told that it's okay to be wounded and that people are better for their scars.

It wasn't that these people were giving me wrong or bad advice. They cared for me and were basing their comments on what they knew to be true. To them, I was acting crazy and irresponsible. But I felt I had to go despite what I was being told. In hope, I believed God had shown me how to deal with my grief, and I needed to "step out of the boat."

I think of another story from the Bible when I reflect on that time. This one is from the Gospel of Matthew.

In chapter 14, there is a story where Jesus had finished feeding a massive crowd with limited resources.

As soon as dinner finished, Jesus told His followers to get into a boat and head across the lake. He wanted to stick around to ensure that the people he had fed were sent home.

After everyone had left, Jesus went up into the hills to pray. He prayed for quite a while because the story says that when He was done, "Later that night, he was there alone…" (Matthew 14:23).

Having gone ahead of Him, the boat was far from the shore and by this time, a storm had risen. Once again, the disciples found themselves out on the water. It was dark, and the wind and waves were knocking them around.

But instead of having Jesus in the boat with them this time, they were alone. Or were they? Because "Shortly before dawn Jesus went out to them, walking on the lake" (Matthew 14:25).

It freaked the disciples out. You'd think they were used to events like that. All the miracles they had seen, and it wasn't as if Jesus hadn't dealt with storms before. Still, they thought He was a ghost, and they cried out in fear.

Jesus responded by assuring them that it was Him and they didn't have to be afraid. Peter replied, "If it's you, tell me to come to you on the water."

Jesus said, "Come."

Now, I don't know about you, but that seems crazy to me. It's not like the ship was sinking. At least, that's not recorded in the story. So being in a vessel was much safer than stepping out of a boat. But Peter answered the call despite the fact it was a rule-breaking, nature-bending, audacious move. The other guys in the boat must have thought he had lost it.

But he did it anyway. It was against the rules—way outside of the norm. He thumbed his nose at the very laws of nature. He ignored the best advice where storms and boats were concerned, defying gravity.

I felt like Peter—walking on water—as I began my healing journey.

A Storm on the Interstate

On the way to Grand Rapids, a nasty storm tested my resolve.

As I neared the city, the sky opened up, and it began to pour. The rain came in waves, and the water blanketed my windshield. I couldn't see much beyond the hood of my van. I put my windshield wipers on the fastest setting, which wasn't enough.

To make matters worse, I was driving in a construction zone. The lanes compressed as concrete barriers squeezed three lanes of traffic into two. The lines on the road were almost invisible. I had only the concrete wall on my left as a guide to where the road was going.

I was stuck in the fast lane and couldn't merge to the right because transport trucks were flying past me. The sheer force of the draft they created threatened to flip my vehicle over. They kicked up a spray that only made matters worse. Add to that the puddles that sent a flood onto my windshield. I was in a pitched battle to keep my car on the road.

It was dangerous and frightening. I felt disoriented. Panic rose from the depths of my soul. My eyes clouded, and I was having difficulty breathing. I wondered if I would survive this bout with grief.

Torrential rainfall, squeezed in by concrete barriers on one side and fast-moving transports on the other, I was unable to see what was ahead of me and worried about what might be coming from behind. With nowhere to pull over, I was crying like a baby while hurtling down the Interstate; and my heart was breaking over and over. A tsunami of grief hit me hard and threatened to wipe me out.

I was running the gauntlet, buffeted on all sides by hazards and nature, and I thought I would die.

So I cried out to God. "Help me! What do You expect me to do now?" I said, "Are You going to kill me here on the road to Grand Rapids?"

He said, "No."

I cried, "What do You expect me to do?"

And He said, "Give thanks."

Exasperated, I cried, "For what? Lorraine is gone. What am I going to do? I don't know what to do. I have five kids at home. I don't know what to do. I'm stuck here in this storm. I don't know what to do. I. Don't. Know. What. To. Do."

And again, He said, "Give thanks."

Only this time, He added "For Theo … and Justin … and Kara … and Nick … and …"

And it dawned on me. Just as God had whispered "You are mine" after my daughter, Cherie, died, He had spoken words of life to me in this dire situation. He was there, and He told me what to do. God had not forsaken me. He would not let me come to ruin. And the hope that comes from gratitude began to rise in my soul.

I picked it up from there. I began thanking God for Theo, Justin, Kara, Nick, Karissa, Michael, Lara, Jayme, and Elissa. I gave Him thanks for the time I had with Lorraine. I gave thanks for the person I had become because of her influence in my life and for all the good things we had shared. I thanked God for all the blessings in my life.

As I began to thank God for past joys and the blessings that remained in my life, the storm began to subside.

And as the storm subsided, the construction zone ended.

Something broke in those moments. That "something" was the cord of grief that bound me up. I was able to breathe. A palpable calm settled on me, and I knew what I needed to do when pain "came in like a flood."

I would "raise a standard" of gratitude and praise. Gratitude for the great gifts given and praise to the Giver of the gifts.

Let the Son Shine In
In hindsight, I believe God led me to a window as I travelled to Grand Rapids. He showed me that I get to make a choice. When I chose gratitude and praise, I opened the curtains, cranked open the window, and let the sunshine in.

The alternative? Shut the window and draw the curtain. Shut myself away from God and my family, friends, and community. Who would have blamed me?

I chose hope. Part of my calling has been to choose between letting the sunshine in or drawing the curtains.

Healing on the Interstate
Within a few miles of the construction zone ending, I was able to pull over into a rest area. I parked the van and took a bit of time to gather myself. Not since the bodysurfing incident in the Philippines had I feared for my life that way. Not since breaking through the water's surface had I felt such relief.

Once my hands stopped shaking, I took a deep breath and remembered why I was there in the first place.

I wiped my tears, put on my signal light, merged onto the Interstate, and continued on my way.

The healing I needed and desired began out on I96—as I drove through the storm to Grand Rapids.

My healing would come through gratitude. My frame of mind would change when I gave thanks.

Composure replaced panic.

I was able to breathe.

I experienced a new level of peace.

And I was not afraid.

I had hope.

Healing would come.

I spent a couple of days in Grand Rapids. I was able to walk where Lorraine and I had walked in the early days of our relationship. I got to visit with family and old college friends. I was able to take a break and catch my breath.

I had prayed that God would heal my heart. Not with twine and tape, but in a way that left no scars. I knew this was the only way I would be able to raise my children.

My healing began—where Lorraine and I started our journey together—and I knew I would be able to move on ahead from there.

Walk on the Water

Before I wrap up this story, let me go back to Jesus and Peter walking on water.

My experience on 196 reminded me of the way that story played out.

Peter accepted Jesus's invitation. He got out of the boat, and Scripture tells us he walked on water toward Jesus. But he began to sink after becoming distracted by the wind and waves. Terrified, he cried out, "Lord, save me!" (Matthew 14:30).

The story says that "Immediately Jesus reached out his hand and caught him" (Matthew 14:31). Then they climbed into the boat together.

When I reflect on my trip to Grand Rapids, I see a direct correlation between my experience and Peter's.

Like Peter, I had ignored the circumstances and stepped out in faith. Like Peter, I lost courage and began to sink into despair. Like Peter, I had to be immediately rescued. And like Peter, I was able to walk on water with Jesus. The wind and waves could no longer bowl me over because I was walking on top of them.

I love this story for many reasons. But the biggest reason I love it is that I see the ever-present, gracious, and loving character of Jesus in it.

I love that Jesus acted with immediacy when Peter called out. I love that He caught Peter and walked back to the boat with him. Jesus didn't carry Peter like a child. He didn't drag Peter through the water, half-submerged, to remind Peter and everyone else of their lack of faith. He didn't vault Peter over His shoulder and carry him fireman-style.

He caught Peter. Then the two of them walked to the boat. Not because Peter needed rescuing, but because that is where Jesus wanted to go in the first place. Peter walked on water with Jesus as Jesus moved toward His desired destination. That's awesome.

When I broke down during the storm, God didn't rebuke me. Instead, He took me by the hand and led me to gratitude. Sure, He rescued me, and I am glad that He did. But I walked away, healed and strengthened because of how God dealt with me.

Like Peter, He showed me that He is ever-present, gracious, and loving.

Wade in the Water

In my life, there have been many storms. They came with suddenness and surprise. I had no control over when and where they occurred.

Storms produce powerful effects, like waves that can overwhelm and debilitate. I've found myself in situations where I was out of my depth and gasping for air.

But I've learned that wading into the water is a forceful pushback against the waves. You can find solid footing if you approach with purpose and caution and lean into the wave.

Even in the storms of life, when the waves come crashing down, there's hope.

Choose hope. Choose pushback.

Wade in the water.
God's gonna trouble the water.

And there, you will find healing for your heart, soul, and mind.

You might even find you're on top of the wave that threatened to wipe you out.

Chapter 8

Speaking of Waves

Mightier than the thunder of the great waters,
mightier than the breakers of the sea—
the LORD on high is mighty.
(Psalm 93:4)

Once upon a time, there was a man who had many children. He knew what it was like to herd cats.

Not only did he raise lots of kids, but he had children who had gone on to glory before him. He knew what it was like to be a childless father.

This man had been fatherless for a significant period of his childhood because his father had been killed suddenly and tragically. He knew what it was to be a fatherless child.

And like his mother before him, he had been widowed, for he had lost his wife to cancer. He knew how it felt to have his heart torn out.

The man could empathize with the dispossessed because he had been forced to leave his home.

He knew what it was like to be displaced because he had been destitute.

This man was well acquainted with sorrow.

He seemed to suffer some measure of loss and grief at every turn.

And yet, that isn't the theme of his story.

The Author had something else in mind.

The Rest of the Story

Perhaps the greatest miracles in life are ones that fly directly in the face of sorrow, sickness, and sin.

For my family and me, the greatest miracle looks like this.

God brought renewed hope into our lives in the form of my wife, Jessica. And with her would eventually come Catherine and Bella, which brings the tally to fourteen children—for those of you who were keeping score.

Not only does she love me, but she is "Super Mom."

God healed our broken hearts and provided the family with a mother who would love the kids as her own. Did I mention that she's "Captain Marvel"?

In Jessica, God gave me a wife, partner, and helpmeet. He heard my prayers, healed my heart, and filled it with love for this remarkable woman.

Talk about a turnabout. When God acts on our behalf, heads turn.

There's a love story worthy of a Hollywood script here, but I'll save that for another day.

Wave after Wave

While visiting Hawaii, Jessica and I stayed at a resort right next to the ocean. The salt air was refreshing, so we opened the sliding glass door and left it like that for the entire visit.

One of the things that struck me was the relentless nature of the waves. We fell asleep and awoke to the sound of the pounding surf. Sure, there were high and low tides, but the waves kept coming. Awe-inspiring force is on exhibit in the pounding ocean surf. It leaves me breathless even as I think about it.

We played in the waves, as I had all those years ago in the Philippines. They were as powerful as ever. The surges had the power to knock me over, and the rip tide could quickly sweep me away.

If I dwelt on it, the potential for danger and harm could leave me paralyzed with fear. In the grand scheme, I am powerless against the force of the sea. When I looked out at the horizon and thought about its scope, I realized how small I was and how easily I could get lost at sea were I to be swept away by it. I could wax philosophical about how insignificant I am compared to the ocean's vastness.

And yet, that's not how I feel after all these years.

Instead, the vastness of the vista before me caused my heart to think about how big God is and how great His love is toward me. I pondered how God would be with me even in the expansive ocean. He always knows where I am and how I'm doing. I was reminded of Psalm 139, where David wrote,

> If I rise on the wings of the dawn,
> if I settle on the far side of the sea,
> even there your hand will guide me,
> your right hand will hold me fast. (Psalm 139:9–10)

He holds me. God is strong when I am not. "My power is made perfect in weakness" (2 Corinthians 12:9).

Hope in God has allowed me to survive the onslaught and thrive in the aftermath. I cling to Him, and I know He has held me when I can't hold on any longer. I'm safe in God's loving and capable hands. I'll never be lost because He is always with me.

> Jesus, Saviour, pilot me
> Over life's tempestuous sea;
> Unknown waves before me roll,
> Hiding rock and treach'rous shoal.
> Chart and compass come from Thee.
> Jesus, Saviour, pilot me.
> (Edward Hopper)

I love how The Message communicates Luke 1:50: "His mercy flows in wave after wave on those who are in awe before him."

May you experience mercy that flows in wave after wave, and may you know relentless hope. May you stand in awe before Him.

In doing so, may you be "Unbroken."

About the Author

Terry Posthumus is a man of many talents. He is a GMA-nominated recording artist, a World Vision Artist Affiliate, and an innovative singer-songwriter. He is a talented animator, having worked with notable companies such as Disney Animation, Keyframe Digital, and DNEG. He is also a tenured college professor teaching animation at Humber College in Toronto. He is husband to Jessica and father to Theo, Justin, Kara, Nick, Karissa, Michael, Lara, Jayme, Catherine, and Bella. Terry loves spending time at the cottage and days of whimsy—going on adventures with his crew searching for the consummate off-the-beaten-path donut shops.

OTHER TITLES BY
CASTLE QUAY BOOKS

Ann McCallum

A *Holy* CALLING

Becoming A Godly Wife

CASTLE QUAY BOOKS

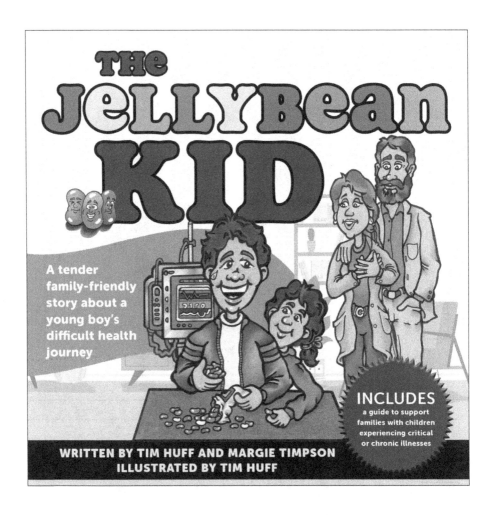

DEBT REDUCTION

WITH TOM COPLAND
(Chartered Professional Accountant)

*Biblical Principles to Deal With
Inflation, High Interest Rates,
and Eliminating Debt*

CASTLE QUAY BOOKS